GUITAR *signature licks*

BEST OF Aggro-METAL

by
Troy
Stetina

W9-CEZ-063

Guitar for cover image provided by Cascio Music.

ISBN 0-634-02341-1

HAL•LEONARD®
CORPORATION

Visit Hal Leonard Online at
www.halleonard.com

Contents

INTRODUCTION

These days, music seems to resist easy genre classification more than ever. Bands are constantly exploring, blending styles and sounds in order to break new sonic ground. So what exactly is modern metal? That's a good question, and it's not so easy to answer simply. To get a better understanding of the current state and direction of metal against the ever-changing musical backdrop, let's take a brief look at the evolution of hard rock and metal to see just what has brought us up to this point.

More than anything else, it's all about *tone*. Guitarists often think in terms of scales, notes, patterns, or rhythms, but we cannot forget the fact that the tone (the sound itself) trumps all of these finer aspects. No other quality is so immediate, or has as much impact as tone. It's the first thing that a person—musician and music fan alike—will notice about music.

Heavy metal was born of distorted guitar. Some call it overdrive, fuzz, dirt, grit…but by any other name it's just as sweet. More than any other single thing, it is distorted guitar that supplied the energy of metal—starting all the way back with Jimi Hendrix in the late 1960s. By 1970, distorted guitar powered the music of the early "heavy metal" groups Led Zeppelin, Black Sabbath, and Deep Purple. In the mid and late 1970s, AC/DC, Kiss, and Van Halen further defined the hard rock/heavy metal guitar tone. In the 1980s, classic heavy metal as we've come to know it reached its zenith with bands like Judas Priest, Iron Maiden, Dio, and Ozzy Osbourne—who split from Black Sabbath and went solo. In the process, he created one of the most enduring heavy metal legacies the world has seen—one that has grown to nearly mythic proportion. We also saw rise of shred and mastery of the technical side of lead guitar in the late 1980s with Joe Satriani, Steve Vai, and Yngwie Malmsteen. Yet through all of this, the basic guitar tone that powered it all changed relatively little—until Metallica came along.

A new underground metal scene began stirring in the mid 1980s and gradually picked up speed. Birthed by Metallica, Megadeth, Slayer, and Metal Church, hyper-speed thrash metal would soon burn out, but it's characteristic "mid-scooped" tone would live on. Metallica slowed their tempos while keeping their revamped tone intact and ultimately came to rule over the Second Coming of metal. For the nearly twenty years of metal that preceded, the distorted guitar tone had occupied essentially the midrange area of the tonal spectrum. The "scooped" tone changed that, giving a heavier and clearly more aggressive sound, and in the process effectively gave a new lease on metal.

The third significant advent arrived in the mid 1990s and has since come into full force with a new crop of metal bands like Korn, Limp Bizkit, Sevendust, Machine Head, Soulfly, Fear Factory, and others. Modern metal is about low tunings. The first band to experiment with low tuning was in fact Black Sabbath (way back in 1974), but they were ahead of their time, and low tuning went by the wayside. In the 1990s, however, new bands—eager to find a sound that would differentiate them—revisited the altered tunings pioneered two decades earlier and took the concept a step further.

Aided by modern amplifier technology as well as modern recording technology, low tunings today have the distinct advantage of an almost unlimited EQ ("equalization" of the tonal spectrum) adjustment. So instead of quickly sinking into a dark tonal abyss where notes become impossible to distinguish, the guitar tone can now be made to convey these ultra-low notes better to the listener. Of course, the lowest tunings will still to some degree suffer a bit of extra "flapping" and difficult-to-hear, pitch-killing lowness, but that's part of the charm!

Modern Metal Tone

First of all, of course, we're talking massive distortion for the most part, with clean guitar tones employed occasionally as a dynamic tool. At the risk of stating the obvious, I'll briefly summarize the concepts and methods involved here, as this is basic to all the songs and tones throughout this book. In modern amplifiers, the distorted sound is a result of pushing a preamp volume (gain level) to the point of clipping the circuit. A master volume then controls the overall volume level of that distorted sound. (Some amps have a third, or even a fourth gain stage in between these two.) A distortion pedal may also be used ahead of the amp's first gain stage to give an even more saturated distortion quality. Most guitar effects processors incorporate distortion as well, effectively replacing the "distortion pedal." To facilitate changing between different sounds—a distorted tone vs. a clean tone—many amps incorporate channel switching. Effects processors accomplish the same thing using presets. Whatever type of gear you are using, it is assumed that you can accomplish an appropriate level of distortion or a clean tone as necessary and switch between them. Therefore, nothing more about distortion or a clean tone will be said unless it significantly departs from the norm.

The use of guitar effects is pronounced in modern metal, as the ongoing search for strange and ever more differentiated soundscapes continues. Most often, these tend to be one of two types: pedal-controlled effects like wah-wah or volume pedals, and the pitch-based effects chorus, flange, and phase. A third category of effects—reverb and delay— is used sparingly. Ideally, you should have either some foot-pedal "stompboxes" to accomplish these effects or a good multi-effect processor that includes an expression pedal. Whenever effects are employed, I will explain the critical effect parameters needed to create the general quality as well as the specific unit I used. Keep in mind that it isn't necessary to get the exact same effect model I'm using—you only need something similar. But even if you don't have the effect, you can still learn the part. It just won't sound quite the same.

In terms of EQ, modern metal guitar is all over the map—from scooped "thrashy" tones to strong midrange presence. But all these familiar tones seem to be reinvented when applied to low tuning—the guitar just doesn't sound the same when it's down a whole step, or two, or three, or four! Great pains have been taken on this audio CD to duplicate as close as possible the actual recording's tones, and I have attempted throughout this book to give you insight as to the exact nature of the EQ of each band's guitar sound. If this gets too technical, or simply is beyond the ability of your amp to emulate, don't worry about it; you can certainly play all songs leaving your amp settings unchanged. The tunings, however, are a must. Let's take a quick tour of the various tunings employed throughout this book.

Modern Metal Tuning

First, we will consider standard tuning and its slacked variations. After standard tuning, the second tuning shown below is a slacked tuning with all strings lowered across the board evenly by one half step. This E♭ tuning has been around a while, and was in fact quite commonly used throughout the '70s and '80s. In this case, the low E string is actually sounding an absolute pitch of E♭, but we don't re-learn all the note names on the fretboard. We still call it an E—and notate it as an E—but with the awareness that we are playing with all pitches sounding a half step lower. The songs in this book also utilize a slacked D tuning and "super-slacked" B tuning, down one step and two and a half steps, respectively. In each case, all chord shapes on the guitar remain intact; they just sound a little (or a lot) lower. And in each case, the lowest note is still referred to and written as if it were an E even though its true pitch is lower. Tunings are shown from low to high.

Standard Tuning:	E–A–D–G–B–E
Down 1/2 Step (E♭ tuning):	E♭–A♭–D♭–G♭–B♭–E♭
Down 1 Step (D tuning):	D–G–C–F–A–D
Down 2 1/2 Steps (B tuning):	B–E–A–D–F♯–B

The next tunings are based on Drop D tuning. Here, all strings are tuned to standard pitch except the lowest string, which is lowered one whole step to D. Since the relative interval between the lowest string and the others is now different, all chord and scale shapes will change to compensate for this. We now refer to and notate the open low sixth string as a D—it's no longer a low E string—and we must revisit all the note names on that string. (Shift each note name up two frets.) Then come the slacked variations of Drop D. Just as we saw before with slacked tuning, slacked variations of Drop D continue to utilize the same note-naming scheme as regular Drop D, with the caveat that all strings are simply lowered across the board by the appropriate amount. So we continue to label and notate the sixth string as a D regardless of its true sounding pitch. Songs in this book use Drop D itself as well as the slacked versions Drop D down one step and Drop D down one and a half steps. Note: Drop D down one and a half steps lowers the sixth string to the absolute pitch of B. This is the most common tuning used in this book.

Drop D tuning:	D–A–D–G–B–E
Drop D Down 1 Step:	C–G–C–F–A–D
Drop D Down 1 1/2 Steps:	B–F♯–B–E–G♯–C♯

Drop A tuning reaches down even further. It is similar to Drop D, except that instead of lowering the sixth string just a whole step to D, it is lowered all the way down to A—a distance of seven half steps below standard tuning! All remaining strings stay in standard tuning. This has the unique quality of creating octave intervals between strings 5 and 6. In Drop A tuning, we notate the low A string at its correct absolute pitch of A.

Drop A tuning:	A–A–D–G–B–E

Now for the seven-string tuning. Standard tuning for a seven-string guitar is like a six string with an additional low B serving as the seventh string. In this case, we always refer to and notate the low string just as it truly is—an ultra-low B note. This might seem a bit confusing at first, due to the fact that it is in fact the same pitch as the six-string tuning down two and a half steps and Drop D down one and a half steps, yet in those cases we notated it as an E and D, respectively (because they are evenly slacked from standard and Drop D). Now, we are notating it as a B. But if you trace the tuning approach as presented above, you'll see why this little dilemma arises. The standard seven-string tuning is not a slack tuning, so we notate it at its absolute pitch. This is just something with which you'll want to become familiar. But just when you've got a handle on that, whack! Along comes the slack-tuning version of seven-string tuning: down one step. Following our tuning logic, we continue to notate the seventh string's pitch as a low B, even though the actual sounding pitch is down to A. Will the insanity ever end?

7–String Tuning:	B–E–A–D–G–B–E
7–String Down 1 Step:	A–D–G–C–F–A–D

Okay, that's it for the tuning…or is it? What do you do when you don't happen to have a seven-string guitar lying around? Time to twist those tuning pegs again. Provided you don't have to play anything on the highest string, you can just tune strings 1–6 of your six-string equal to strings 2–7 of a seven-string, or B–E–A–D–G–B. This is in fact the preferred tuning of Coal Chamber, one of the featured bands in this book. Notice the similarity of this to the standard slack tuning down two and a half steps shown earlier in the first tuning group above. (Only the second string is altered one half step.)

| 7–String tuning on a six-string: | B–E–A–D–G–B |
| 7–String Down 1, on six-string: | A–D–G–C–F–A |

Finally, we need to discuss the mechanical requirements of such a variety of tunings. When a string is slacked to a lower pitch, it begins to flap around a bit more. Some of that is fine. In fact, it's more than fine—it's very cool. But when the tension loosens beyond a certain point, the pitch can become excessively unstable. Tuning is troublesome and intonation may become problematic. (Intonation is the aspect of being in tune at all the different positions on the fretboard from low to high.) You'll need to use heavier string gauges for the lower tunings in order to maintain a reasonable string tension.

For standard tuning and slacked variations down one whole step as well as Drop D, normal extra-light (.009), light (.010), or medium (.011) gauge strings are likely fine. For Drop D down one or down one and a half steps, a medium-heavy gauge set—or medium with extra heavy bottom—is appropriate. For the lowest tunings such as the seven-string tunings on a six-string guitar, or standard down two and a half steps, a heavy gauge works best.

This hints at a problem you may encounter while working through this book, should you happen to have only one six-string guitar: If you set up your guitar with heavy gauge strings to play the lowest tunings, you're likely to have serious problems when attempting to tune all the way up to standard tuning for the two songs that use it later in this book. This is because the tension differential between a heavy and light gauge string set in standard tuning is so different that it would likely require truss-rod or other adjustments to keep the guitar playing properly and the action reasonable. You have several options:

1. Get another guitar! String one for low tunings, the other for higher tunings.
2. Set up your guitar for the lower tunings and learn them first, then restring with a lighter-gauge for higher tunings.
3. Put on a medium-gauge set with a heavy bottom and hope for the best!

"Offbeat" Sixteenths

Another signature element of modern metal lies in the rhythmic aspect. While '70s and '80s metal tended to feature rhythms in eighth-note based accent patterns, the '90s has ratcheted it up a notch, favoring more complex sixteenth-note accents. First explored in '70s funk, sixteenth-note "offbeats" now comprise the meat of modern metal rhythm guitar. And therein lies the primary difficulty in performing this music well.

Therefore, throughout this book, significant effort has been devoted to explaining the rhythmic aspect of this music. Simply put, playing the notes at "about the right time" isn't enough. Ideally, you want to feel the underlying pulse (or beat) in your whole body at the same time that you play "against" it. Without a strong and accurate sense of the underlying pulse at all times, these ultra-cool rhythms will quickly disintegrate into mush! Pay attention to the specific picking advice as well as other details given in each song's prep section.

THE SONGS

The songs appearing in this book are the following:

"Southtown"—from *The Fundamental Elements of Southtown*, P.O.D. (Payable On Death)
"Sugar"—from the self-titled debut, *System of a Down*
"From this Day"—from *The Burning Red*, Machine Head
"Faith"—from *Three Dollar Bill, Y'All*, Limp Bizkit
"Spit It Out"—from the self-titled debut, *Slipknot*
"Denial"—from *Home*, Sevendust
"Bleed"—from the self-titled debut, *Soulfly*
"Loco"—from the self-titled debut, *Coal Chamber*
"Edgecrusher"—from *Obsolete*, Fear Factory
"Come Original"—from *Soundsystem*, 311
"Pardon Me"—from *Make Yourself,* Incubus
"Testify"—from *The Battle of Los Angeles*, Rage Against the Machine
"Welcome to the Fold"—from *Title of Record*, Filter
"When World's Collide"—from *Tonight the Stars Revolt!*, Powerman 5000

THE RECORDING

On the accompanying audio, the featured guitar part is isolated in the right channel, and the backing tracks and/or other supporting guitar parts are isolated in the left channel. By using the balance control on your stereo, you may isolate the guitar part for learning purposes, hear the full band, or play along with just the backing tracks. Of course, you may also fine-tune it to hear exactly the relative blend of instruments that you desire. Great care has been given to recreating the tones for each song accurately within the context of this unique stereo spread. So get ready to rock! This CD is going to push your rhythms to the breaking point and beyond!

Guitars, bass, and synth:	Troy Stetina
Drums:	Scott Schroedl

Recorded, mixed, and mastered at Artist Underground, New Berlin, Wisconsin. Engineered by Mike Wenz. Produced by Troy Stetina.

ABOUT THE AUTHOR

Troy Stetina is a world-renown guitarist and leading music educator. He has written more than 25 books and methods for Hal Leonard Corporation including *Speed Mechanics for Lead Guitar, Metal Rhythm Guitar Vol. 1* and *2*, and *Metal Lead Guitar Vol. 1* and *2*. Troy is also a contributing writer for *GuitarOne* magazine. His latest CD is *Exottica*. Visit him on the web at http://www.stetina.com.

SOUTHTOWN

Words and Music by Noah Bernando, Paul Sandoval, Mark Daniels, and Marcos Curiel

Figure 1–Intro, Verse, Interlude, and Chorus

Payable On Death (aka P.O.D.) is a band with a message and a mission—literally. Standing well apart from the rest of modern metal content, this faith-based group promotes messages of common love, respect, and spiritual conviction in the face of hardcore reality. Formed in 1992, this band from L.A.'s south side (an area known as "Southtown") consists of Marcos (guitar), Wuv (drums), Wuv's cousin Sonny (vocals), and bassist Traa (who came on board a year later). After relentless touring and selling 30,000 of their independent, self-financed CD *Brown*, P.O.D. eventually landed a deal with Atlantic Records in August, 1998. Their 1999 Atlantic release, *The Fundamental Elements of Southtown* is the initial result.

In terms of guitar tone, it begins with a clean intro. Then massive distortion is the order of the day. This author mimicked the original tone by going through a Boss distortion pedal, then into a Line 6 POD (how appropriate, eh?) digital software modeling pre-amp. The POD was set to a Dual Rectifier simulation (MESA/Boogie) with the drive on 10. The midrange EQ is strongly present, along with significant high frequency "bite" (4k-6k).

The tuning is down one whole step. This slack tuning is also sometimes also referred to as "D tuning," since the low sixth string of the guitar drops from its standard pitch of E down to D. But keep in mind that all strings are dropped equally across the board. Because all the fretboard intervals remain intact (and therefore chord and scale shapes stay the same), we don't re-name all the notes and chords on the guitar neck. So before going any further, let's tune up (or perhaps more accurately, *down*, in this case).

 Track 1 (low to high): D–G–C–F–A–D

The central riff of "Southtown" is essentially the alternating, two-chord progression G5–E5 with added B5 "pivot points" placed in between. This results in the power chord pattern G5–B5–E5–B5. Rhythmically, the riff punches hard with a relatively busy sixteenth-note groove. Specifically, a sixteenth/sixteenth/eighth figure is followed by two offbeat sixteenths. (*Offbeat* sixteenths refer to those found on the second and fourth subdivisions of the beat.) Then, the two-beat rhythmic motif begins to repeat on beats 3–4, but morphs into four sixteenths on the B5 chord for beat 4.

To play this well, you should maintain a consistent alternate-picking format. This means you alternate downstrokes and upstrokes of the pick, skipping any unplayed subdivisions without your overall momentum. This is really a strumming format applied to a sixteenth-note rhythm and power chords. The pattern should be down/up/down, up, up, down/up/down, down/up/down/up.

A brief two-measure interlude acts as a temporary break before the pounding chorus riff enters. Further enhancing the "departure" effect here, the entire mix is flanged. The direction "w/ pick and fingers" means that you should pick the lower string and use your middle finger to pluck the higher notes (in this case found on the third string).

The chorus is built upon the same tonal construct as that found in the verse riff, but stripped a bit more to its "fundamental elements." The B5 pivot chords fall away and we see the G5–E5 motion more starkly. By the way, you may also notice a subtle, alternating light/dark feel or quality as this chord movement washes back and forth between relative major (G) and minor (Em) tonal centers. Beats 2 and 4 of each measure color each chord with a ninth tone, effectively implying a progression of Gsus2–Em(add9). Rhythmically, the chorus also simplifies—the sixteenth/sixteenth/eighth figure becomes double eighth-note punches—and the syncopation falls away to reveal consistent sixteenths on both beats 2 and 4 without fail.

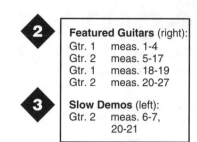

Featured Guitars (right):
Gtr. 1   meas. 1-4
Gtr. 2   meas. 5-17
Gtr. 1   meas. 18-19
Gtr. 2   meas. 20-27

3
Slow Demos (left):
Gtr. 2   meas. 6-7,
          20-21

Fig. 1

Tune down 1 step:
(low to high) D–G–C–F–A–D

Intro
Moderately ♩ = 112

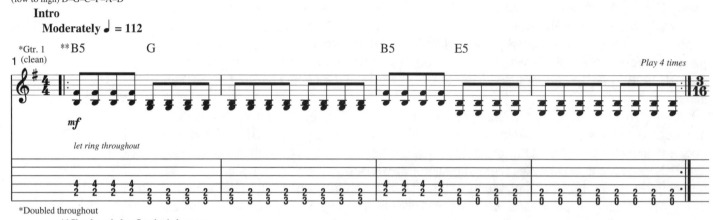

*Doubled throughout

**Chord symbols reflect basic harmony.

Slower ♩ = 81

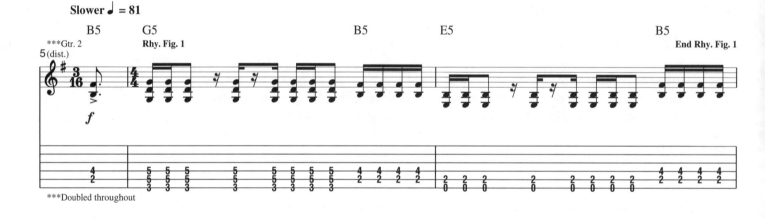

***Doubled throughout

Verse

Gtr. 2: w/ Rhy. Fig. 1

Gtr. 2: w/ Rhy. Fig. 1 (4 times)

1. Wel-come to   hard times,   back a - gain _ like it's nev - er been. For the
2. One   love   it's eas - i - er said than done.   Can I

first time,   seems to mess _ with my head. _ So when I re - a - lize   what it takes,   can I re - late   with what-
rise a - bove   ev - 'ry-thing   that's in my way?   Like words you say,   you let your tongue get   loose _ and when

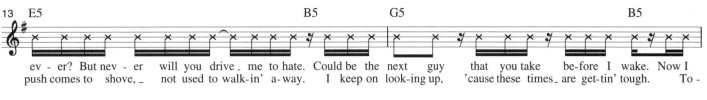

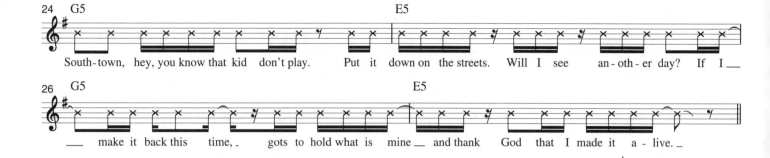

Figure 2–Bridge

The bridge goes a little nuts with the special-effect noise. Underneath, clean guitars dominate. Amidst sustained harmonics (Gtr. 4), the featured part (Gtr. 1) plays a single note line E–F#–G—the first three notes of the E minor scale—but with a twist. The E note is displaced downward by one octave. Both guitars employ an amp-produced tremolo effect, common on older Fender-style amps, which creates a constant "down-up" wavering of the volume.

After two measures, a clean melody line enters (Gtr. 5). On the audio, this part is centered in the mix to help separate it as well as possible as an alternate featured part should you chose to play it instead of Gtr. 4. In the melody itself, a strange repetitive quality is apparent, even as it simultaneously seems to evade clear repetition. What's going on here? Over Gtr. 4's repeating one-measure phrase, the melody is a *six-beat* phrase, which cycles over and over, sometimes coinciding with the underlying guitar's phrase and other times splitting it in half.

Heavy guitars enter in measure 9, picking up on the E–F#–G motif established earlier. Here it appears in power chords. After the second three-note group, muted "clicks" with a syncopated sixteenth rhythm cap off the one-measure phrase.

4 Featured Guitars:
Gtr. 1 (right) meas. 1-8
Gtr. 2 (right) meas. 9-20
Gtr. 5 (center) meas. 3-9

5 Slow Demos:
Gtr. 2 meas. 9-10

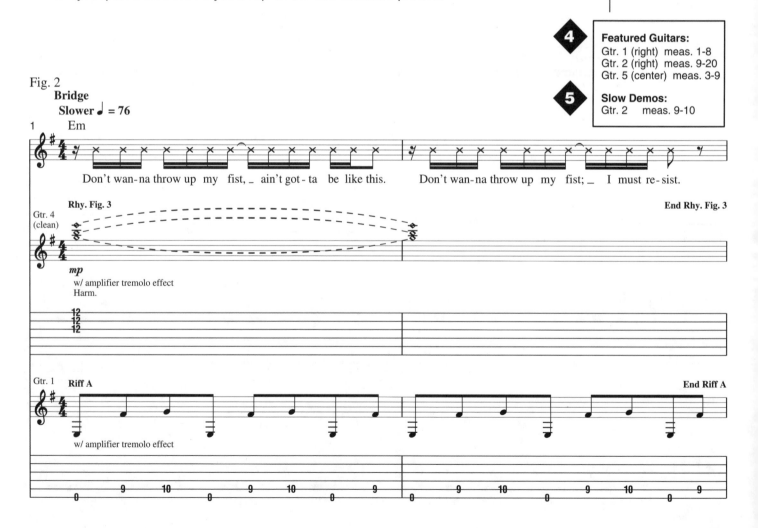

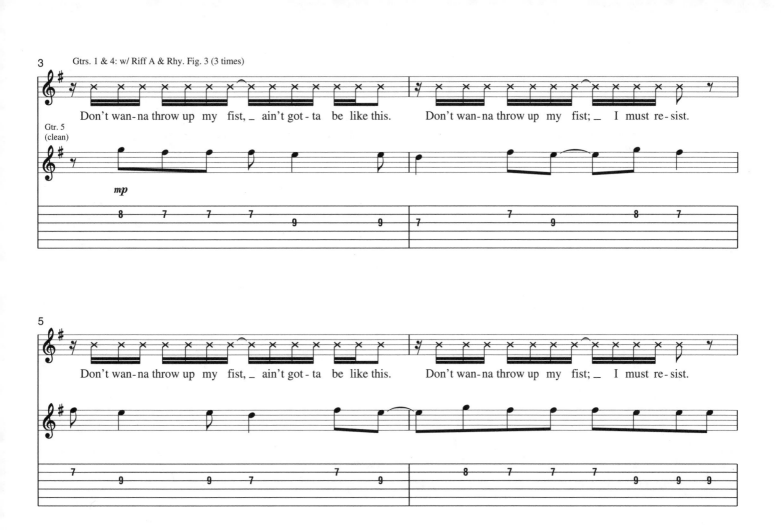

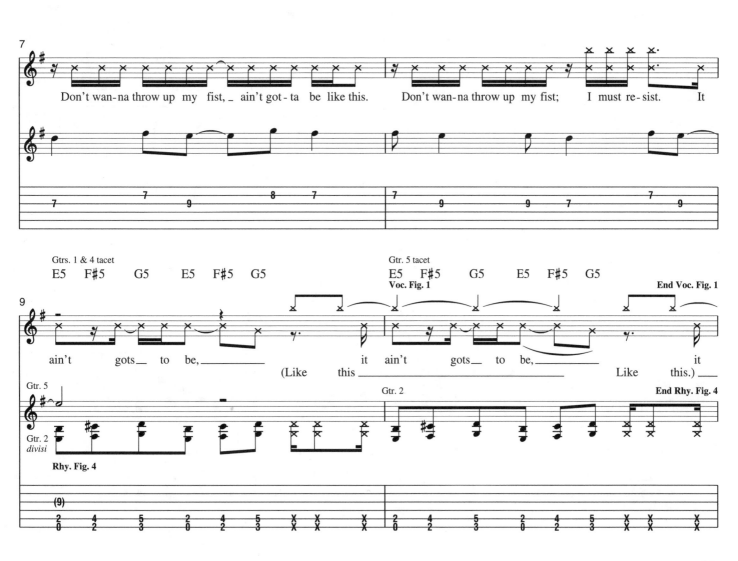

Bkgd. Voc.: w/ Voc. Fig. 1 (5 times)
Gtr. 2: w/ Rhy. Fig. 4 (2 times)

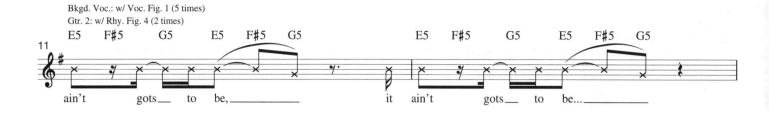

ain't   gots__ to be,_____   it ain't   gots__ to be...___

Life   ain't sup-posed to be like   this. __   Life   ain't sup-posed to be like   this. __

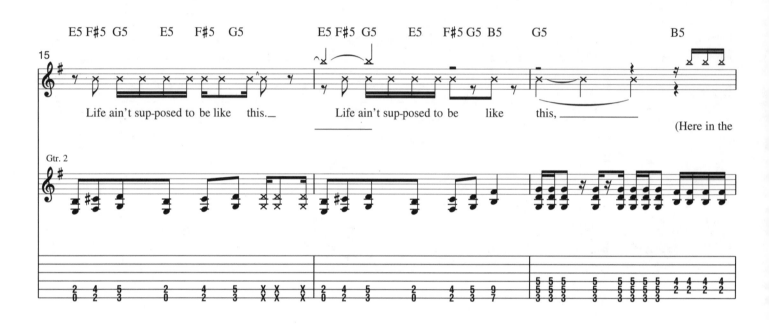

Life ain't sup-posed to be like   this.__   Life ain't sup-posed to be   like   this,_____

(Here in the

Gtr. 2

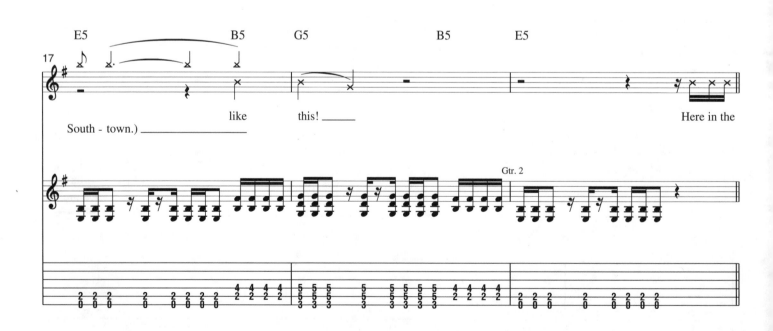

like   this! _____

South - town.) _____   Here in the

Gtr. 2

12

SUGAR

Words and Music by Daron Malakian, Serj Tankian, Shavo Odadjian, and John Dolmayan

Figure 3–Chorus, Verse, Chorus

System of a Down is the collaboration of four American-born musicians from L.A. that share one relatively unusual characteristic—they are all of Armenian heritage. Serj Tankian (vocals) and Daron Malakian (guitar) met in 1993 as their two bands shared the same rehearsal studio. Shortly thereafter, they united under the name Soil. After several lineup changes, including the addition of Shavo Odadjian (bass) and John Dolmayan (drums), System of a Down was finally born in 1995. Amid lyrical assaults ranging from the personal to aggressive political and social indictments, SOAD draws upon an unusually wide range of stylistic influences including rap, jazz, hardcore, goth, Middle-Eastern, and even Armenian music. Dynamics can change on a dime. Vocalist/lyricist Serj explains, "We don't just concentrate on an aggressive sound, though we have that. Anger becomes more angry when you're quiet at first." Nowhere is that better exemplified than in "Sugar," the third cut from their self-titled 1998 debut.

First, a word about the tone: More than any other band in this book, the guitars in "Sugar" have a pronounced lower midrange peak in the 600-800 Hz range. Most amplifiers tone controls center in the ballpark frequencies 100 Hz for bass, 1 kHz for mid, and maybe 5 kHz for treble. So, unless your amp is blessed with a graphic EQ, the best you can do is to crank up the mid control and keep the bass and treble somewhat backed off. In addition, many amps have a so-called "presence" control, which is generally a shelving EQ that boosts or cuts frequencies above 1 kHz, all the way up to the high end. You might try either backing the presence off, or pushing it up and backing the treble off to compensate.

The tuning is *Drop D down 1 step*, which lowers the sixth string to an absolute pitch of C. From the previous song's ("Southtown") tuning, this is accomplished simply by lowering the sixth string down one whole step and leaving all other strings unchanged. If your guitar happens to have a floating vibrato bar, you'll still have to go through the entire tuning process a few times, however. (This is because floating vibrato systems balance the string tension against several springs. When you lower the pitch and tension of one string, the entire bridge floats downward slightly to find a new equilibrium point, and therefore sends all the other strings slightly sharp.) As always, we ignore the equally slacked portion of the tuning, and regard all the notes on the neck as if we were playing in Drop D tuning.

 Drop D Tuning, Down 1 Step: C-G-C-F-A-D

The chorus is centered upon the simple four-chord motif, D5–A5–A♭5–G5, grinding away repeatedly in eighth-note power chords in a decidedly heavy, somewhat punk-inspired way. Also notice the characteristic "one finger" power chord shape that emerges in Drop D tuning (and all its slacked variations). Play all downstrokes. Then, just about when you get used to it, the guitar drops out, and the four-note motif undergoes a sudden transformation. Now in the context of a bass line and swing rhythm on the ride cymbal, it changes abruptly from balls-out heaviness to light jazz!

The verse is peppered with short bursts of higher-register notes. The first two pitches, A/F, effectively spell out the fifth and minor third of a Dm chord. The next two notes are E/C, followed by A/D. This is the fifth, minor third, and root of Am, which pulls to resolve itself back to the tonal center, D. Listen for the implied chordal motion Dm–Am–Dm (i–v–i) and its characteristic resolution.

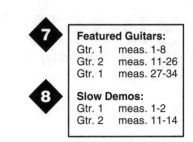

Fig. 3

Drop D tuning; down 1 step:
(low to high) D–A–F–C–G–C

Chorus

Moderate Rock ♩ = 138

*doubled throughout

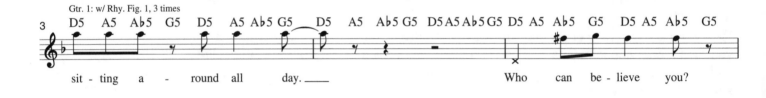

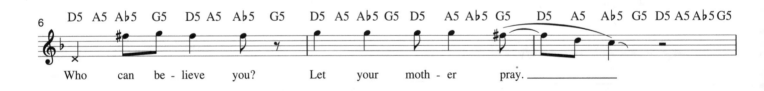

Double-Time Feel   **Interlude**

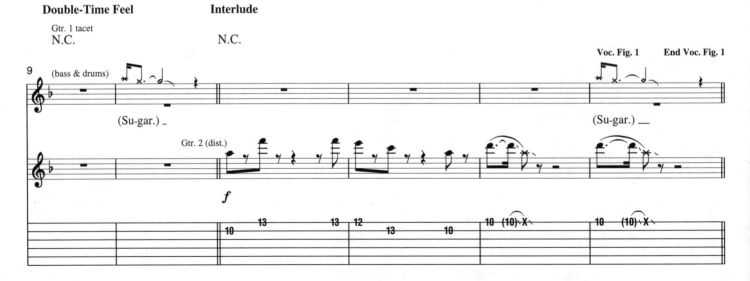

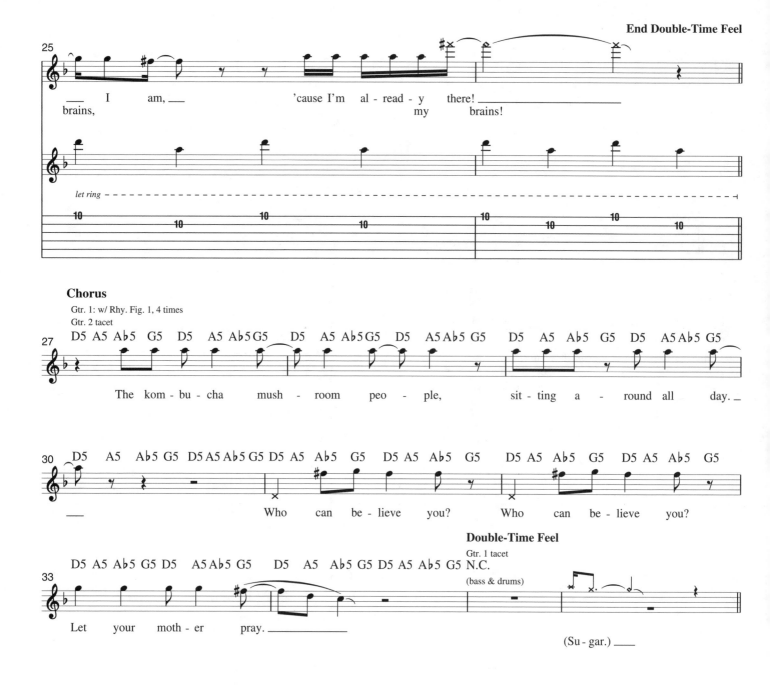

Figure 4–Bridge and Outro

The bridge undergoes an abrupt tempo change. It may be a bit easier to catch this if you count it in double time (with the hi-hat in the breaks as the new pulse). Then, the tempo can be considered to increase from about 140 bpm up to roughly 180 bpm. To make your chord "jabs" sharp and clean, mute and stop the strings with both hands—not just the right or the left alone.

The outro embellishes upon the basic accent points first established in the bridge. The sixteenths are best played with a down/up/down/up picking pattern. Even though the speed at first lends itself to the possibility of all downstrokes, a gradual *accelerando* (speeding up of the tempo) eventually results in quite a challenge when the speed reaches the 180 bpm ballpark.

At measure 17, we break back into the song's original chorus motif but at critical velocity. Full palm muting here allows the energy level to rise yet higher, continuing the gradual crescendo effect right up to the end as the palm mutes are opened in measure 20. The tempo also continues to rise right up to the end.

FROM THIS DAY

Lyrics by Robert Flynn
Music by Machine Head

Figure 5–Intro

Hailing from the San Francisco Bay area, Machine Head is down-tuned, extreme metal blending a decidedly melodic edge with rap in a high-energy mix. The four-piece formed in 1992 with Ahreu Luster on guitar, Robert Flynn on vocals and guitar, Adam Duce on bass, and Dave McClain on drums. Shortly thereafter, the group's 1994 effort, *Burn My Eyes*, would prove to become the top-selling debut album in the history of Roadrunner Records, while the follow-up release, *The More Things Change*, cemented their presence among the leaders of the new, crushingly brutal "aggro-rock" style. For their third release, 1999's *The Burning Red*, the band joined forces with producers Ross Robinson (Korn, Limp Bizkit) and Terry Date (White Zombie, Deftones, Soundgarden). "From This Day" is the first single of the album.

The tuning is Drop D down one and a half steps. This is just like the previous song's tuning, except the strings are tuned down another half step across the board. So, the absolute pitch of the sixth string falls from C down to a super-low B. However, as this is another "across the board slack tuning," we continue to notate and refer to this low note as a D, while at the same time understanding that all pitches are sounding one and a half steps lower.

 Drop D Down 1 1/2 Steps: B–F#–B–E–G#–C#

The key factor here is the effects, beginning with the wah pedal of Gtr. 1. I used a Digitech XP100 (set to patch 04) and rocked forward and back in an eighth-note pulse. Added to this is a subtle cycling chorus quality, which I achieved with the Leslie cabinet simulation effect on the Line 6 POD. A fast amp tremolo set to a fairly light level may also achieve a similar pulsing result.

The tone itself is slightly scooped, giving a somewhat thick, bassy quality. It also has a fair amount of high-frequency definition. But it's not a real "scoop" in that the midrange is still quite present—a bass-treble boost may be a more accurate description. A relative tonal setting of bass up, mids flat (12 o'clock), and treble up should do the trick. Keep the presence fairly backed off. I used the POD setting "Brit Hi Gain" (emulating a Marshall JCM 800).

Over the pitch center of D, the opening measure spells out the D Locrian mode (D–E♭–F–G–A♭–B♭–C). After anchoring beat 1 on the open D5 power chord, we see the twisted melody emerge as E♭ (♭2nd), D (root), B♭ (♭6th), D (root), C (♭7th), and A♭ (♭5th). The next measure throws in a surprise C# (major 7th), drawing upon the strong melodic tension found just a half step below its target resolution (D). This marks the midpoint of the phrase. The third measure repeats the pattern of the first measure. Then, the fourth and final measure wraps up the full phrase with a higher-octave bend and release, A♭–B♭–A♭ (♭5th–♭6th–♭5th), again returning to the promised land of the "metallic" Locrian mode.

At measure 15, things jump into high gear as Gtrs. 1 and 2 come together in unison on the sixth string. Sixteenth-note syncopation abounds in the repeated sixteenth/eighth/sixteenth figures. Pick each with a down/up/pause/up motion. The notes D–F–A♭ (root, ♭3rd, ♭5th) form a D diminished arpeggio and again are drawn from the pitches of D Locrian. Notice the fast chromatic passage at the end of measure 18, which completes the new four-measure phrase.

Fig. 5

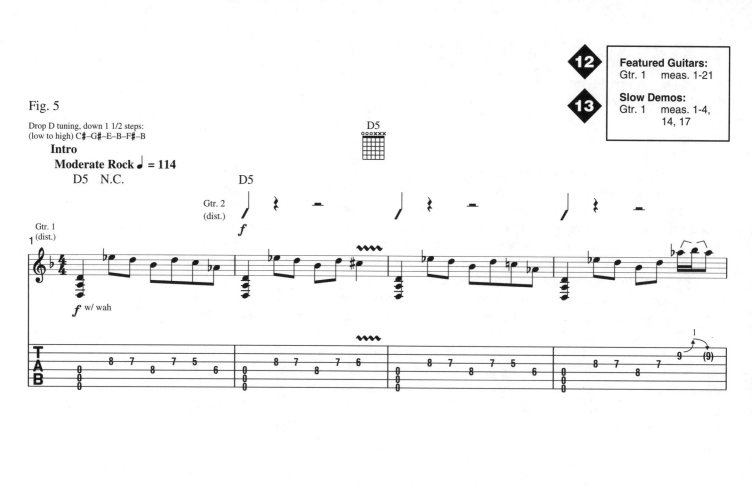
Drop D tuning, down 1 1/2 steps:
(low to high) C#–G#–E–B–F#–B

Intro
Moderate Rock ♩ = 114

Get up!

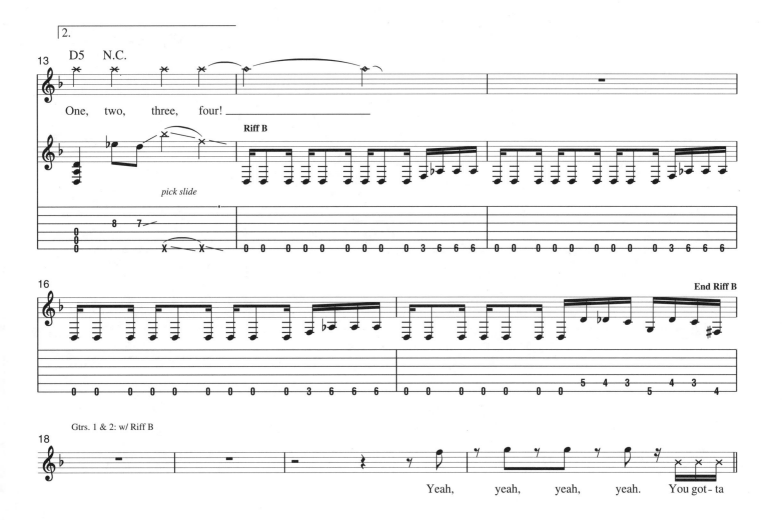

Figure 6–Verse and Chorus

The verse raps over sporadic low note attacks, leaving plenty of space so the listener can focus primarily on the vocal part. The first two notes are simply a pair of eighth notes. Then you stop the string for a moment of silence on beat 2 until the fourth sixteenth subdivision requires another note. Beat 3 starts with a short eighth rest, followed by two sixteenths. Standard sixteenth alternate-picking format would indicate you should pick this down/down…up…down/up. However, when significant space exists in a rhythm, the picking pattern may be altered without any deterioration of timing accuracy. And often in such cases, a different stroke may be preferred simply because down and up strokes of the pick sometimes just sound different. If memory serves, I believe I tended to pick this section via a down/up…down…down/up pattern.

After four measures of verse, a new guitar enters with the wah pedal. Start each measure with the pedal fully backed off, rock forward into beat 2, back into beat 3, and forward again into beat 4. Left hand mutes and octaves dominate the part. For octaves, use your first and third fingers to play the two notes, allowing the underside of your first finger to lightly touch and hold the intervening string quiet.

The chorus recalls the low unison riff from the intro. But after one measure, it moves the rhythmic motif through a chord progression, rather than keeping it statically attached to D. At its core, the progression is essentially Dm–F–B♭–C (i–♭III–♭VI–♭VII), which acts to support the vocal melody and helps give it a stronger sense of direction and resolution. This is somewhat uncharacteristic for the super heavy modern metal styles, and therein lies Machine Head's prominent "melodic edge." (Actually, if played at a higher tuning and with a more simple rhythmic interpretation, this progression is quite at home in many '80s melodic rock tunes!) But with all the band's aggressive madness, low-tuned riffing, and rhythmic sophistication, "From This Day" clearly rocks at the forefront of modern metal.

14 Featured Guitars:
Gtr. 1   meas. 1-4
Gtr. 3   meas. 5-12
Gtr. 1   meas. 13-20
Gtr. 3   meas. 21-22

15 Slow Demos:
Gtr. 1   meas. 1-2
Gtr. 3   meas. 5-6
Gtr. 1   meas. 13-16
Gtr. 3   meas. 21-22

Fig. 6

Verse

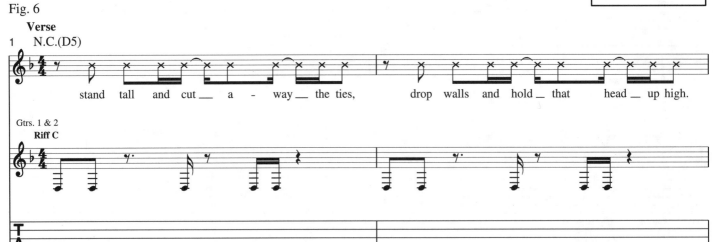

stand tall and cut _ a - way _ the ties,   drop walls and hold _ that head _ up high.

Gtrs. 1 & 2
Riff C

The world is fast and youth _ ain't gon - na wait,   so grab hold be - fore _ it gets _ too late.

End Riff C

Gtrs. 1 & 2: w/ Riff C

Bare your soul and strip _ a - way _ the cold   of with-ered life, that past _ so grey, _ and old.

Gtr. 3 **Riff D**
(dist.)

mf
w/ wah-wah

End Riff D

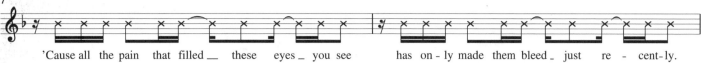

Gtr. 3: w/ Riff D (2 1/2 times)

'Cause all the pain that filled __ these eyes __ you see has on - ly made them bleed __ just re - cent-ly.

Tears that made __ me a-shamed to be __ me, but that gave __ me strength to see __ me, made a spark __ that lit the dark __ and

Chorus

Gtr. 3: w/ Fill 1   Gtr. 3 tacet

let me shine. Time to see, be - lieve this __ in me, this

Gtrs. 1 & 2

Rhy. Fig. 1

pain that __ I feel deep __ in - side. _____

End Rhy. Fig. 1

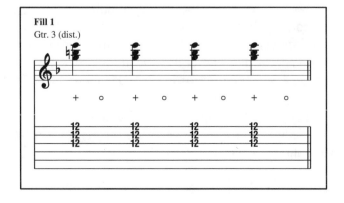

Fill 1
Gtr. 3 (dist.)

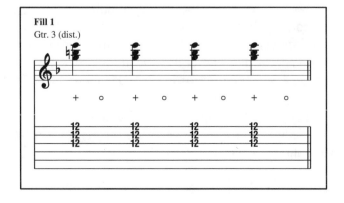

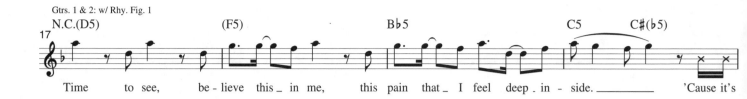

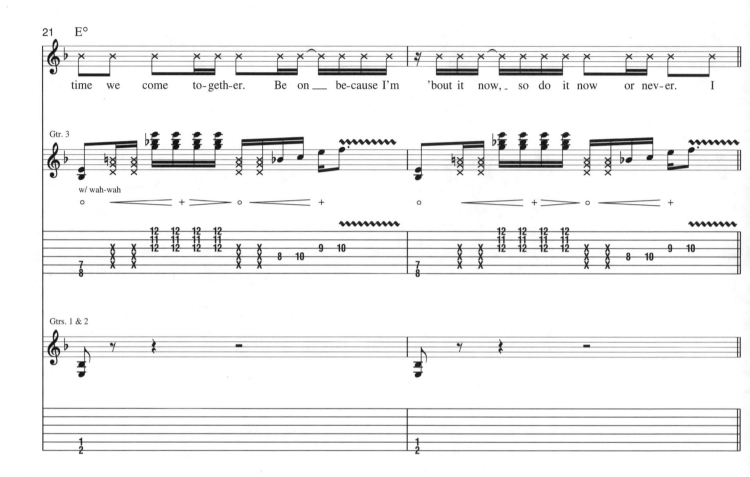

Figure 7–Interlude and Bridge

The interlude section opens with a measure of slicing pick harmonics on the open third string. First, turn the leading edge of your pick downward so that it crosses that string more on the "rounder" side of the pick (always touching the edge and not the wide, flat portion). Then, lay the side of your thumb lightly against that string. Move the pick up and down across the string while continuing to touch the string the whole time with the side of your thumb, and high-pitched harmonics will sound. The exact pitch produced depends on the location of your thumb. Try moving your entire picking hand up and down the string in small amounts near the pickups until you find the right location.

Measure 2 kicks in with a new riff, based on the common metal rhythm figure of dotted-eighth/dotted-eighth/eighth notes. Using all downstrokes is preferred. Notice the familiar riff structure emerge—three repetitions followed by a fourth measure which caps off the full phrase with a different ending. At the end of the second full repetition, beginning in measure 9, a pick scrape intervenes and replaces the first D5 power chord of each measure.

In measure 14, Gtr. 1 enters again with its opening figure and wah'ed tone for an "intro reprise" to act as the bridge section. The energy comes down here for a bit until eventually building back up and into the final chorus.

Fig. 7

*Random pinch harmonics are produced by the right hand thumb lightly touching
the string while gradually moving the pick towards the bridge.

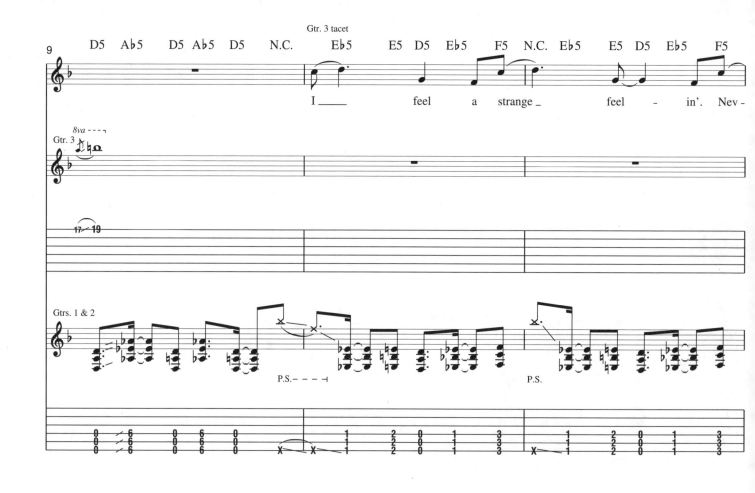

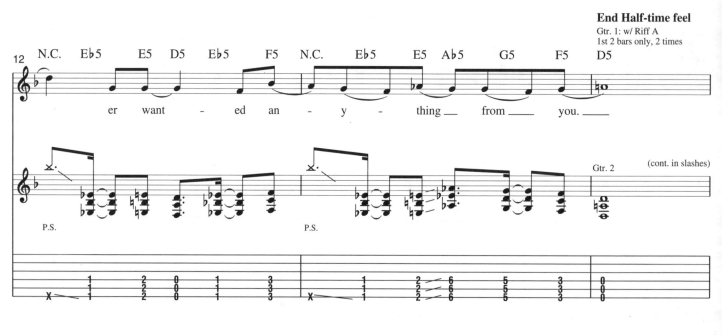

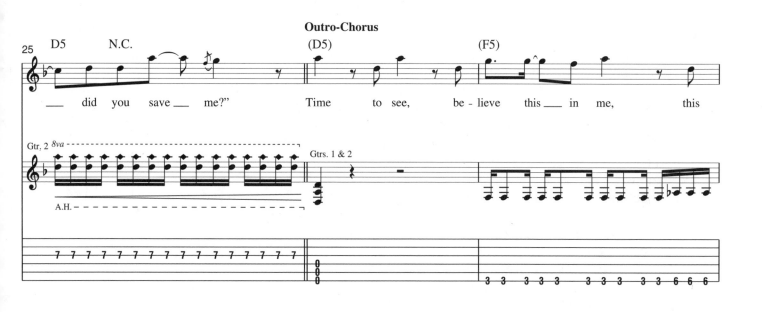

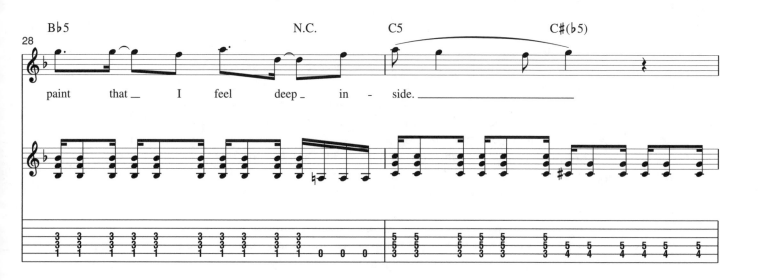

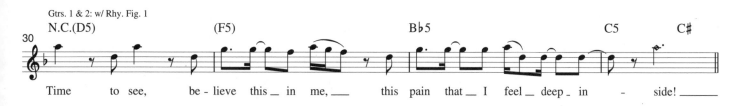

FAITH

Words and Music by George Michael

Figure 8–Intro, Verse, Pre-chorus, Chorus, Verse, Pre-chorus, Chorus

Limp Bizkit has risen to the top of the modern rock world with their distinct, energetic fusion of metal, punk, and hip-hop, and an attitude of offending all equally. The Florida-based band originated in 1994 with Fred Durst (vocals), his friend Sam Rivers (bass), John Otto (drums), and Wes Borland (guitar). Later they added DJ Lethal. Their story of success, like most rock bands, is part hard work and part precipitous timing. While in Jacksonville for a show, bassist Fieldy of Korn got a few tattoos by Fred Durst, a tattoo artist, and the two became friends. Eventually, Korn picked up Limp Bizkit's demo tape and were so impressed, they passed it on to producer Ross Robinson. After touring with House of Pain and Deftones, Limp Bizkit signed with Flip/Interscope and released their debut album, *Three Dollar Bill, Y'All*, in 1997. Amid relentless touring, *Significant Other* came out in 1999, and their latest effort, *Chocolate Starfish And The Hot Dog Flavored Water*, was released in October of 2000.

"Faith" was a blockbuster pop hit by George Michael on his 1987 album by the same name, which sold over seven million copies. Reworked by Limp Bizkit, it's...well, a little different than the original version, with all the rough edges and unmistakable irreverent attitude that mark their work remaining fully intact.

The tuning is Drop D down one and a half steps—just the same as the previous song. Tone-wise, Limp Bizkit goes for a somewhat lo-fi approach. This song opens with a patently unpolished clean tone, strong in the midrange. Later, a chorus effect is kicked on, which brightens the tone a bit. The distorted tone is on the dark side, almost muddy at times: bass up, mid flat, treble backed off a bit.

The clean opening section is all sixteenth-note chord strumming. Keep your picking motion down/up/down/up with each sixteenth subdivision, so your momentum is undisturbed throughout. The mutes are accomplished by releasing pressure in your fretting hand, thereby transforming the chord strike into a muted "click." Play fairly harsh and strong with the picking hand, allowing a little extra string noise here and there, particularly on the low sixth string. These low "notes" are accidental, however, and more a relic of his less than fully muted mutes than any intentional sounding of that low string. The four-measure progression is D–D–C–D (I–I–♭VII–I), spelling out a D Mixolydian tonality.

Notice the tempo fluctuation—slowing down significantly—when the vocal enters in the verse. This "mistake," clearly a part of the band's unpolished charm, is actually identical to the performance as found on the Limp Bizkit recording. It seems only more obvious here because there are no vocals to attract the listener's attention and divert it somewhat from the tempo change. Just get used to the feel of how much to slow down. Later, the tempo picks back up significantly in the pre-chorus.

At the pre-chorus (measure 13), switch on a chorus effect set with the rate slow, the depth fairly high, and the mix at 100%. This tends to change the tone and naturally accentuate the highs. The eight-measure chord progression is C–D three times, followed by two measures on A (V chord). Hold each chord's full shape over each measure, allowing all the strings to ring together. The quick C to D moves at the end of measures 14, 16, and 18 are accomplished by laying your first finger flat to barre the appropriate strings at the fifth fret, then hammering down your third finger flat to barre at the seventh fret.

Heavy guitars enter at the chorus. While the top of the chords can be seen to move from D5 to C5 and back, the lower portion (octave Ds) remains anchored on the tonal center, acting as a pedal tone. At the end of each measure 21–23, octave Ds are struck and pulled slightly to bend and raise the pitch. Pull down just enough to raise about quarter tone—half of a half step.

The second verse applies a palm-muted rhythm technique (with distortion) to the same D–D–C–D progression seen in the previous verse (played clean). While alternate sixteenth picking could certainly be used, the accented chords are stronger if you use something I refer to in my metal guitar methods as "accent picking"—playing each D chord with an upstroke, and each low D palm mute with a downstroke. So the picking should be up/down/down, up/down/down, up/down/down, up/down/down, up. This helps the high note of the D chord stand out prominently and separates it more from the mutes.

The second pre-chorus and following chorus is simply a repetition of the first time through. Then Fred subtly encourages the audience to rise.

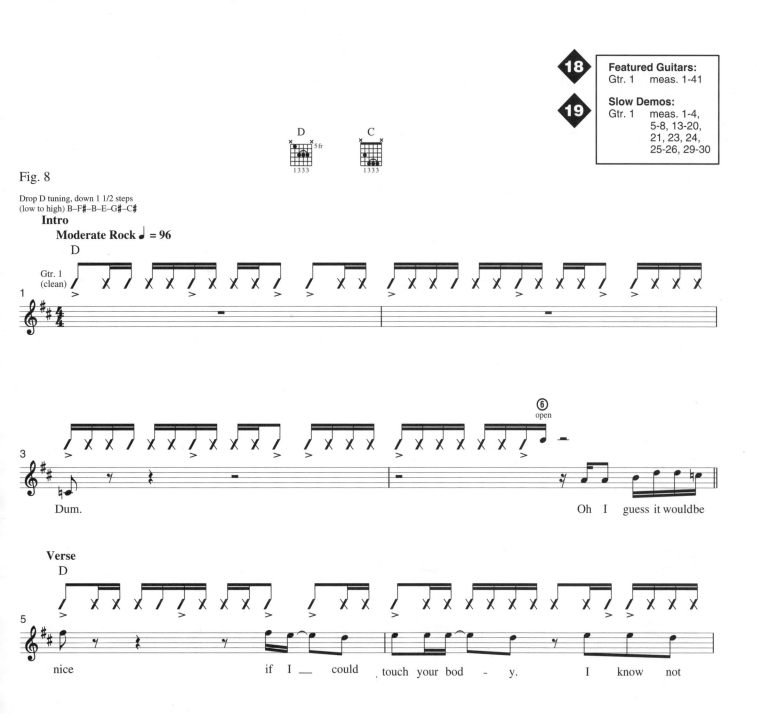

Fig. 8

18 Featured Guitars:
Gtr. 1 meas. 1-41

19 Slow Demos:
Gtr. 1 meas. 1-4,
5-8, 13-20,
21, 23, 24,
25-26, 29-30

Drop D tuning, down 1 1/2 steps
(low to high) B–F♯–B–E–G♯–C♯

Intro
Moderate Rock ♩ = 96

Gtr. 1 (clean)

Dum.

Oh I guess it wouldbe

Verse

nice   if I — could   touch your bod - y.   I   know   not

ev - 'ry - bod - y ___ has got a bod - y like me. ___ But I got - ta think

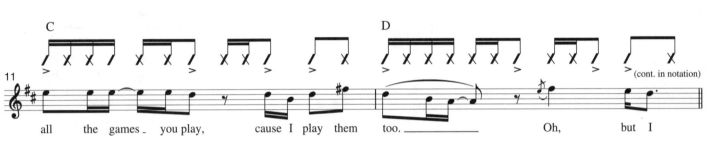

twice be - fore __ I give my heart __ a - way. And I know

all the games __ you play, cause I play them too. ___ Oh, but I

𝄋 Pre-Chorus

need some __ time __ off from the e - mo - tion. Time to
fore this __ riv - er be - comes an __ o - cean. Be - fore you { pick my heart __ off of __ the floor. __

w/ slight dist. & chorus
let ring throughout

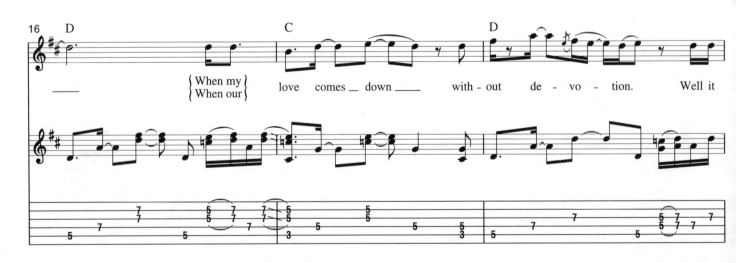

{ When my } love comes __ down ___ with - out de - vo - tion. Well it
{ When our }

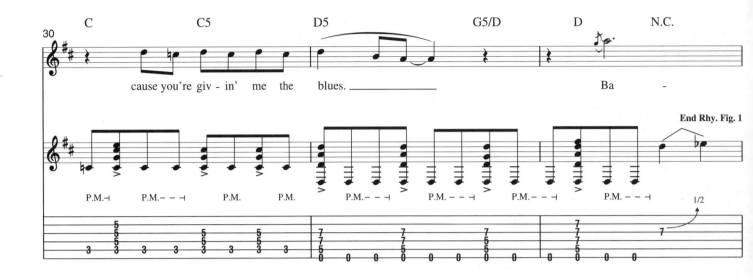

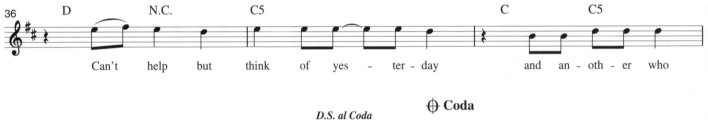

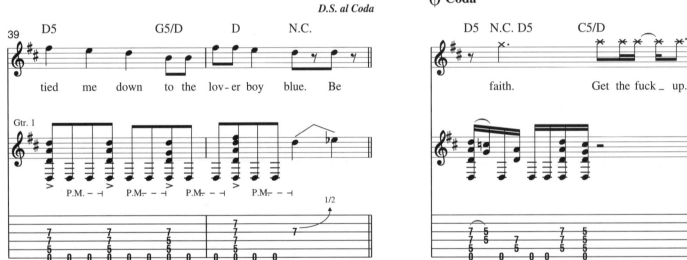

Figure 9–Turntable Solo, Outro

This ending section is pure, writhing Bizkit, as they finally have their own way with the tune without regard to the original in any shape or form. The new riff that emerges is based upon a D–E♭ half step move that draws from a D Phrygian tonality (D–E♭–F–G–A–B♭–C). Rhythmically, we see a two-note repeated pattern tumble against the underlying pulse. Use your available fretting hand to lightly touch and stop the strings during each of the short rests.

In fact, this is actually a signature modern metal rhythmic devise—displacing groups of threes against a timing division set in fours (sixteenth notes). But, you say, there are only *two* chords in each repetition, not three, right? Not so. It's a sixteenth/sixteenth/*rest* pattern. The rest is the third subdivision. Laid together end to end, each group of three lands differently against the underlying pulse and creates the interesting rhythmic quality.

To help get a good feel for this rhythm without losing the connection to the underlying pulse, try picking it down/up, up/down, down/up, up/down/up/down/(pull)/down. This is the pattern as dictated by sixteenth-note alternate picking, which best maintains the overall momentum. After you have that down, however, try it with all downstrokes or as down/up, down/up, down/up, etc.

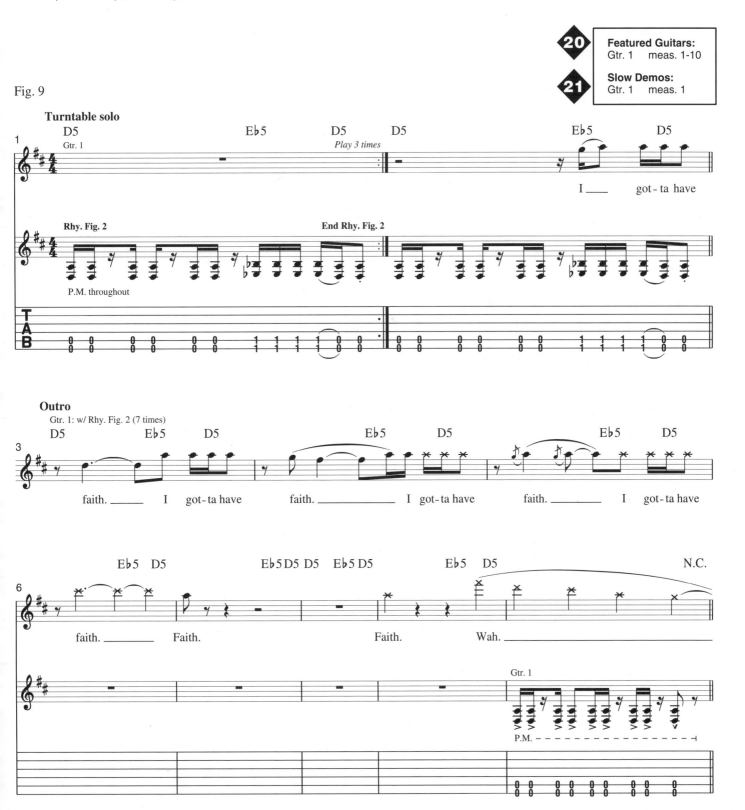

Fig. 9

SPIT IT OUT

Words and Music by Shawn M. Crahan, Paul Gray, Nathan Jordison, and Corey Taylor

Figure 10–Intro, Verse, Chorus

Something threatening out of Iowa? Self-described as "nine freaks from Des Moines," Slipknot is messed up, hardcore, neo-death-metal, horror-hip-hop ultra-violence draped in industrial coveralls and facemasks. At the heart of this "nine-headed savior/destructor of modern heaviosity" is the dual guitar onslaught of James Root and Mick Thomson. Formed in 1995, the group soon thereafter recorded their own self-released effort in 1996, *Mate. Feed. Kill. Repeat.* They signed on to Roadrunner Records through Ross Robinson's I Am Records in 1997, resulting in their 1999 self-titled label release debut.

Track 6, "Spit It Out," utilizes Drop D tuning down one and a half steps, as used in the previous songs. The tone is significantly scooped, but in the *lower* midrange portion of the spectrum—the upper mids are strongly present in the 2–3 kHz range. To get into the ballpark, try the bass up a bit, the mid down, the treble flat, and the presence fully cranked up. Now you're ready for some full-bore rap metal with industrial-edged riff repetition.

Gtr. 1 opens the melee with a repeating one-measure phrase based on a rhythmically displaced three-note motif. E♭5 (♭II) pulls down to the tonic chord, D5 (i), followed by a whole step bend from F (♭3rd) up to G (4th). This spells out a D Phrygian tonality (D–E♭–F–G–A–B♭–C).

A second guitar joins the fray at the verse. Here, the third note of the motif is replaced consistently by high-pitched pick harmonics. Turn the leading edge of your pick down slightly and touch the side of your thumb to the string lightly at the moment you strike the string. Then bend up. Played with all downstrokes at a reasonably fast tempo (144 bpm), this apparently simple riff is deceptively difficult to play well and requires a significant amount of endurance.

The chorus is flat out nuts—sixteenth-note syncopations at high velocity that must tightly interlock with other contrasting rhythmic accents in the lead vocal and crash cymbals. Picking should be: down/up/down, down/up/up, down/down/up, up/down. Try it slowly first, then gradually pick up the pace as you get comfortable with it.

Tonally, the chorus centers upon F, which is the relative major key of D minor. This accounts for the relative brightness heard here. But the pleasantries are discarded promptly with the chromatic insertion of E5 and then E♭5. Note the "sic" happy delirium inherent in the backup vocals—this the brilliant combination of a bright major-key, hook-laden musical delivery mated to a downright ominous lyric, "All I want to do is stamp you out."

A short breakdown interlude enters after the chorus, drawing upon the tritone as a melodic interval (D–A♭). The bend from A♭ (♭5th) up to A (5th) and back down suggests the D blues scale (D–F–G–A♭–A–C).

22

Featured Guitars:
Gtr. 1   meas. 1-6
Gtr. 2   meas. 7-26
Gtr. 1   meas. 27-28

23

Slow Demos:
Gtr. 1   meas. 1-2
Gtr. 2   meas. 7-8,
            19-20

Fig. 10

Drop D tuning; down 1 1/2 steps:
(low to high) B–F♯–B–E–G♯–C♯

Intro

Moderate Rock ♩ = 144

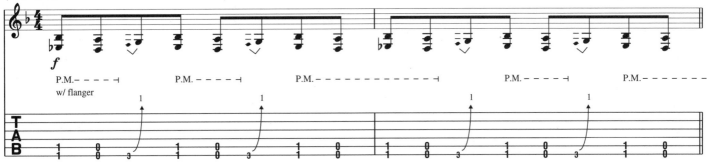

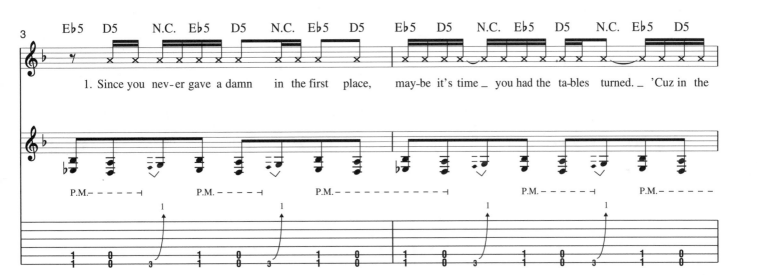

1. Since you nev-er gave a damn   in the first   place,   may-be it's time _ you had the ta-bles   turned. _ 'Cuz in the

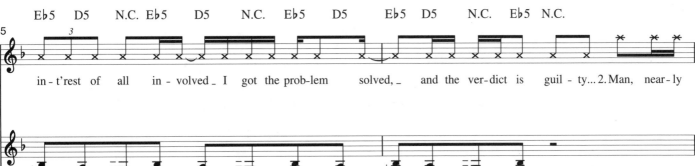

in - t'rest of   all   in - volved _ I got the prob-lem   solved, _   and the ver-dict is   guil - ty... 2. Man, near-ly

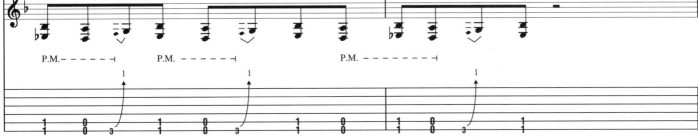

Figure 11–Bridge, Chorus

The bridge features a riff in octaves, which in fact blends together ideas presented earlier in the two previous song structures. The tones D–E♭ (root–♭2nd) come from the intro/verse riff, while the rhythm is that of the chorus. To play octaves, use your first and third fingers, laying your first finger over just enough to touch and mute string 4. Slide your whole hand up and back down without changing your relative finger positions to make the one-fret position shift.

At measure 5, the featured part rises to A–B♭ (5th–♭6th), effectively becoming a harmony in parallel fifths. After two measures, it rises again up to an octave above the original part, to seventeenth position, then abruptly off into space with the "wrong sounding" E octaves in measure 8.

Fig. 11

24 Featured Guitars:
Gtr. 1 meas. 1-8
Gtr. 2 meas. 9-19

25 Slow Demos:
Gtr. 1 meas. 1, 5, 7-8
Gtr. 2 meas. 7-8

Bridge

time I set this rec-ord straight, __ ('cuz) all this nee-dle-nose punch-in' is mak-in' me i - rate.

flanger off

Sick o' my bitch-in' fall-in' on deaf ears. Where you gon-na be in the next five years? The

crew and all __ the fools and all the pol - i - tix. Get your lips read-y, gon-na gag, gon-na make you sick.

DENIAL
Lyrics by Clint Lowery and Morgan Rose
Music by Sevendust

Figure 12–Intro, Verse, Chorus, Interlude

Hailing from Atlanta, Georgia, Sevendust signed with TVT Records in 1996. But things began slowly for the heavy rock quintet, made up of vocalist Lajon Witherspoon, drummer Morgan Rose (husband to bassist Rayna Foss of Coal Chamber), guitarists Clint Lowry and John Connolly, and bassist Vinnie Hornsby. Their 1997 self-titled debut release sold only 300 copies in its first week and took months to reach 1000 units. Nevertheless, through constant touring and strong label support, the word began to spread, and Sevendust struck a resonant chord among modern aggro-metal fans. What began slowly would blossom into a gold record by May, 1999 and cement their position among the leaders of new heavy rock pack. For their sophomore effort, the band sought out veteran producers Toby Wright (Alice in Chains, Korn) and Andy Wallace (Nirvana, Rage Against the Machine). Guest appearances with vocalists Chino Moreno (Deftones) and Skin (Skunk Anansie) also grace the second recording, *Home*, which was released in August 1999. The band's signature ultra-heavy, downtuned riffing and melodic precision populate the disc in equal measure.

The standout track "Denial" is a good case in point. The tuning is Drop D down one and a half steps. The opening progression, smeared with a strong phase effect, later acts as the foundation for the chorus melody amidst a reworked tonal and rhythmic presentation. The first four chords, B5–Cmaj7–E5–D5, seen from the perspective of a B tonal center form a I–♭II–IV–♭III progression. When the upper B note of B5 is held over and into the following C major chord, it creates a major 7th chord—a decidedly delicate-sounding structure that is by any measure unusual in the heavy styles. Over this sonic backdrop, Gtrs. 2 and 3 duel with clashing tones, often sounding a dissonant half step removed. The second four chords are a repeat with the exception of the last, as F♯sus4 (V chord) replaces the D5. A third attempt through the pattern is then aborted on Cmaj7, leaving its unstable, delicate quality to trail off and into unstoppable meanness!

Centered upon D (B minor's relative major), the opening thematic riff pounds hard with its complex, rhythmically displaced sixteenth-note offbeats. The core motif is found in the first four notes: octave D, E, low D, E. Delivered in a highly syncopated fashion, only the first note lands on "solid" rhythmic ground (the downbeat of 1). The following three notes then fall into line on back-to-back sixteenth-note offbeats—the second and fourth sixteenth-note subdivisions of beat 1, then the second sixteenth-note subdivision of beat 2. Picking should be down/up/up/up in order to best maintain your rhythmic momentum. The whole motif lasts exactly one and a half beats.

Now, enter *rhythmic displacement*. We see the entire motif structure repeated so that it falls against the beat differently. Specifically, the starting octave D now lands on the "and" of beat 2 (the "upbeat" of 2)—exactly 180 degrees out of phase. Each following note maintains its same relative timing. After two such patterns, the starting note returns to the downbeat. At this point, we have gone through exactly three full beats, and two motifs. Cycle this whole pattern again and we get four motifs lasting six full beats—the first and third starting on downbeats, the second and fourth starting on upbeats. Finally, two half-step bends act to fill out beats 7 and 8, forming a full two-measure phrase.

Then, as if that's not enough, add to this a slight vibrato on the second note of each motif pattern. Don't pull the string much at all, though. This should be more on the order of a quarter-step bend/release—and that slight bit of bending happens very quickly when the strings are downtuned to this amount. Don't overbend it; just give it a slight "wiggle."

So you now know *what* to do. The only problem remains actually *doing it!* Remember, ideally you want to keep a solid feel of the underlying pulse throughout in addition to playing all the notes. Not easy! Try this first: Tap your foot in double time. That is, tap the pulse at twice normal speed (in eighth notes, not quarters). That places the start of every motif on a "foot tap" and should help a bit. Then, attack it from the other angle, too. Forget about the pulse and just *play the darn thing,* hoping for the best. After enough practice from each of these two approaches, it will eventually fall into place.

The verse uses sporadic chord-slide attacks with huge, double-octave power chords and plenty of open space in between. Notice that the leading edge of each double attack happens to also be the same rhythm as that formed by the leading note of our previous riff motif. That is, the first one starts on beat 1, the second starts on upbeat of 2, the third starts on beat 3, and the fourth starts on the upbeat of 5 (or beat 1, next measure). The tag bends in beats 7 and 8, ripped right out of the first riff ending, further cement this relationship and act to keep the verse riff sounding still quite related to the original.

The chorus runs through the progression established in the intro, with full distortion and a sixteenth-note strumming rhythm. The picking (written beat by beat) should be down/up, down/up/down, up/up, down/down/up for the first two measures (B5–Cmaj7). Continue with the same format. Gtr. 2 splits away into an octave melody for the second half of the chorus.

The interlude takes syncopated sixteenths to the max. Standard alternate picking format says play all sixteenth-note offbeats with upstrokes.

Featured Guitars:
Gtr. 1 (right)   meas. 1-11
Gtr. 2 (center) meas. 1-11
Gtr. 1 (right)   meas. 12-35

Slow Demos:
Gtr. 1   meas. 12-13,
         14-15, 16-17,
         24-27, 28-29,
         30-31, 32-35

Fig. 12

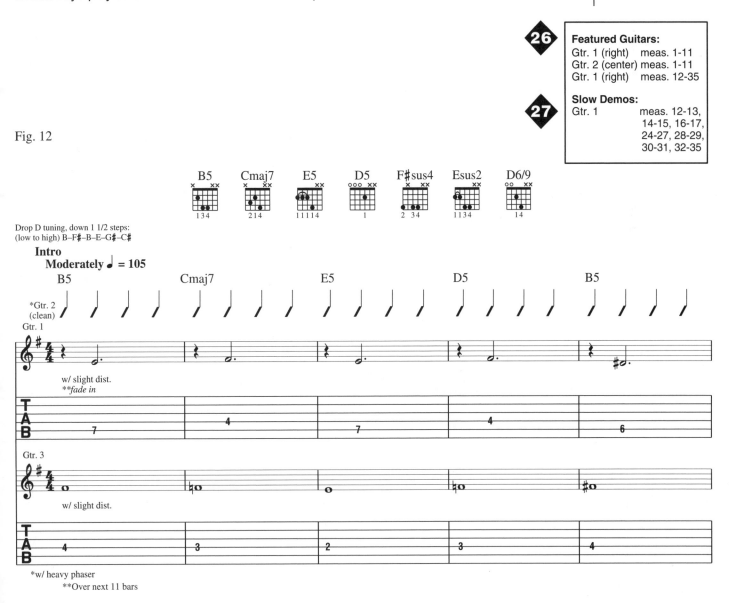

Drop D tuning, down 1 1/2 steps:
(low to high) B–F♯–B–E–G♯–C♯

*w/ heavy phaser
**Over next 11 bars

*Harmony vocal doubles lead vocal an octave lower (next 8 measures).

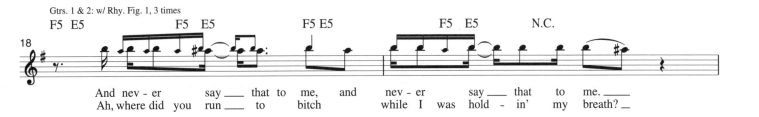
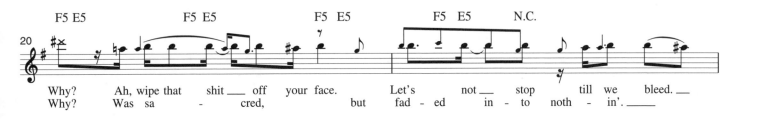
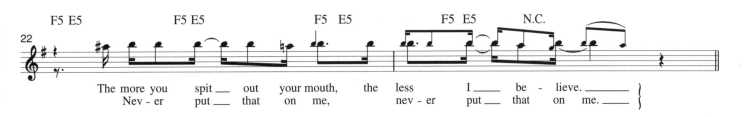
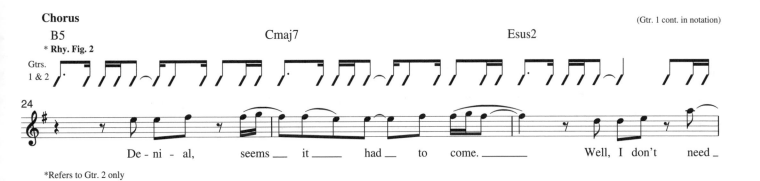
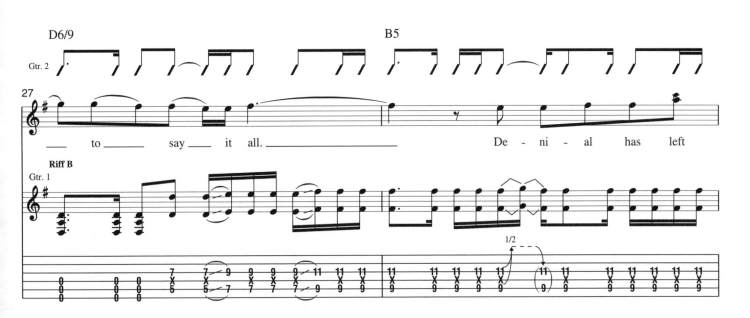

Figure 13–Interlude, Solo, Breakdown, Outro Chorus

Here we have the verse permutation taken down a notch by adding more space. The second and fourth chord assaults are omitted. After playing twice, Gtr. 3 adds a thematic "solo" on top, drawn from a G minor pentatonic shape (G–B♭–C–D–F). A kind of polytonality clash results, as the underlying F5–E5 move is in a world apart. Viewed another way, against the tonal center of D, the solo's notes F–G–B♭–D, actually become ♭3rd–4th–♭6th–root, thus implying D natural minor. Although perhaps more simple, this view overlooks the salient aspect of the music at this point. The rhythm pulls down to E twice, then grounds things on D, while in the intervening "holes," the lead guitar pulls our ear back each time to regard G as a temporary alternative.

The breakdown recalls the intro chord progression, though only in spirit and not verbatim (i.e., the chords are a little different). Things start to heat up again in measures 12–18 as we build back up into a final musical event. Gtr. 2 embarks on a single-note melody, sloshing back and forth between F♯ and E. Harmonically, this is the 5th and 4th of the B5. Over Cmaj7, these tones become the ♯4th and major 3rd. Over E5, we have the 2nd and root. Measure 15 gives a reprieve from the continuum, heading up to G at the half-step bend, followed by a quick trill embellishment and fall to D♯, B's major 3rd. The ending portion of the melody reflects the vocal melody.

28 Featured Guitars:
Gtr. 1 (right)   meas. 1-6
Gtr. 3 (center) meas. 5-6
Gtr. 4 (right)   meas. 7-11
Gtr. 1 (right)   meas. 12-18

29 Slow Demos:
Gtr. 1   meas. 19-26

Fig. 13

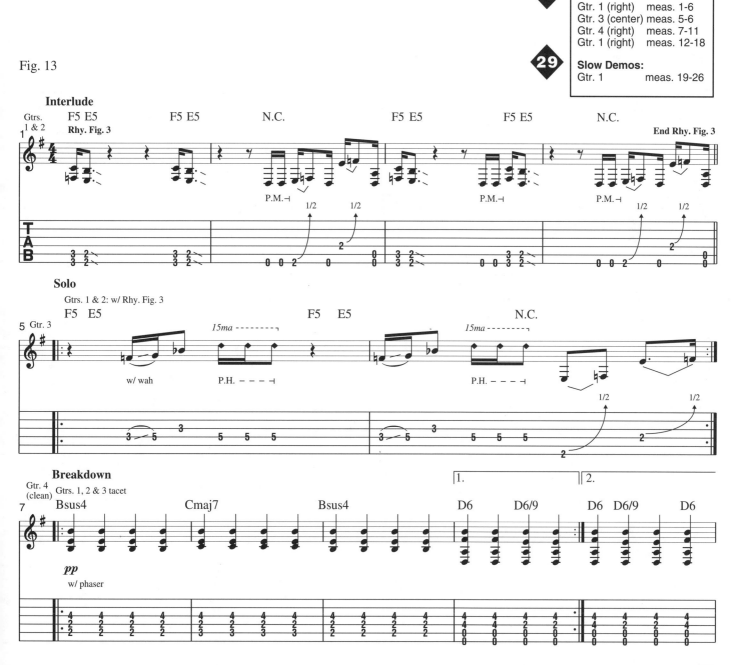

45

BLEED

Words by Max Cavalera and Fred Durst
Music by Max Cavalera

Figure 14–Intro

Arising from Brazil—an area with little support for heavy music at the time—Sepultura had emerged to become one of the most significant metal groups of the late 1980s and early 1990s, pioneering their own distinct fusion of heavy rock and world music. As co-founder and fifteen-year member of that groundbreaking band, Massimiliano ("Max") Cavalera had achieved tremendous success and worldwide acclaim. But things weren't easy or comfortable. In 1996, on the heels of dealing with his own personal tragedy—the unsolved murder of his stepson—Max finally split from Sepultura due to musical and career differences with the other band members.

It was a difficult period, but quitting music was not an option for Max. Organizing his new band Soulfly and writing new music, he poured out his pain, anguish, and frustration into a series of monstrously brutal riffs and lyrics. Under the production guidance of Ross Robinson and mixing talents of Andy Wallace, Soulfly's self-titled debut album was released in 1998. Also joining the fray and enhancing the effort were guest appearances by Fear Factory's Burton Bell, Dino Cazares, and Christian Wolbers, as well as Fred Durst and DJ Lethal of Limp Bizkit, Chino from Deftones, and numerous other musicians.

In "Bleed," the third track of the album, Max unleashes his own torrent of visceral anger and soul-searching condemnation upon the killers of his friend and stepson, Dana Wells, warning of events to come full circle and their ultimate, inescapable conclusion. "What comes around goes around. How long can you live with your soul? When I put your sorry ass in a package, you piece of shit, sealed and delivered…now you sweat because you're goin' down." Fred Durst also weighs in for the chorus "bleeding."

The tuning here is down to a super-low B via standard tuning slacked two and a half steps across the board (the equivalent of five frets). Therefore, we continue to regard and notate the low sixth string as if it were an E.

 Down 2 1/2 Steps: B-E-A-D-F♯-B

The guitars use two different tones. For the clean tones at the start, I used the POD clean setting with the drive (gain, or distortion) raised just enough to give it some grit, then backed off the guitar's volume knob to create a "rounder" and more dull high frequency. A slight amp tremolo effect and slapback delay at about 440 ms were then added. Gtr. 2 also plays through a wah pedal, but it is left in its partially backed-off state until measure 6, when you can actually hear the familiar wah quality for the first time. Other than this one spot, the wah is used as a sort of tonal "filter" of EQ. For the bone-shaking distortion tone, I went for a straightahead dual rectifier (MESA/Boogie) setting on the POD with tone controls at about 6 or 7 on bass, mid, and treble and let the low tuning do its job.

The intro opens with two guitars playing simultaneous two-measure phrases drawn from the E blues scale (E–G–A–B♭–B–D). Notice the signature three-against-four pattern that emerges in measures 4, 6, and 8. After four such phrases, Gtr. 3 fades in on a screaming unison bend technique in measures 10-13, effectively shattering the relative calm. Then things get brutal. Kick on the distortion for the song's main riff at measure 14. The single-note pitches G–F–E (♭3rd–♭2nd–root) imply an E Phrygian tonality.

Featured Guitars:
Gtr. 1   meas. 2-13
Gtr. 4   meas. 14-18

Slow Demos:
Gtr. 1   meas. 2-9
Gtr. 4   meas. 14-15,
17-18

Fig. 14

Tune down 2 1/2 steps:
(low to high) B–E–A–D–F#–B

Intro

Moderate Rock ♩ = 112

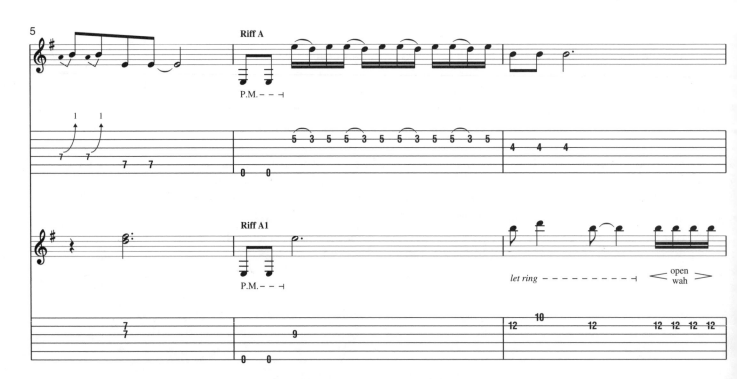

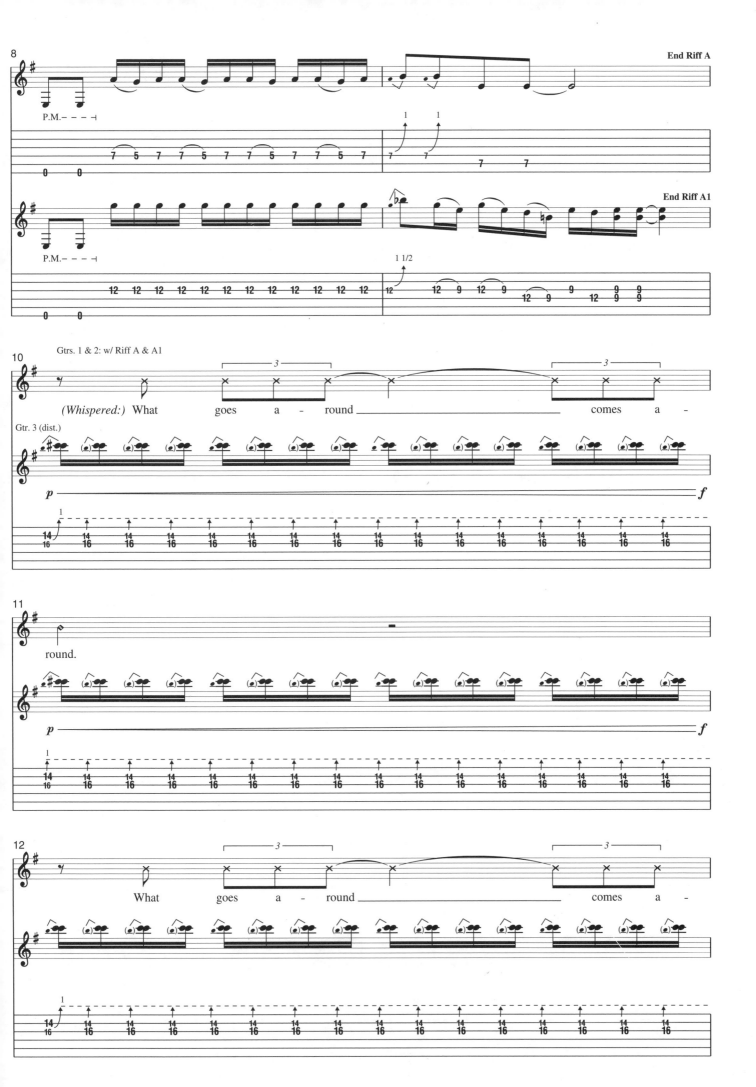

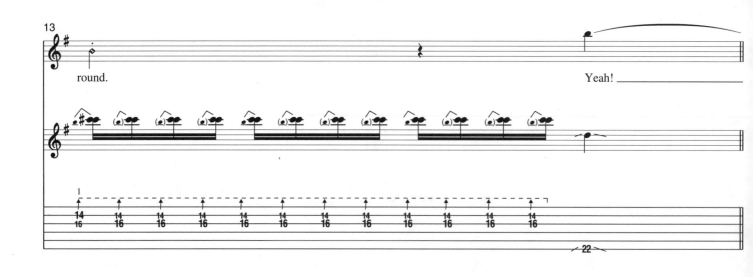

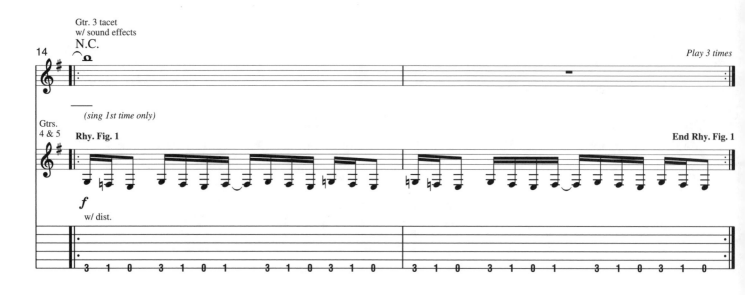

Figure 15–Verse, Chorus

A series of sustaining E5 palm mutes pick up the bass accents and act as a short preamble to the verse. The verse itself uses the previous main riff but at a lower energy level—the guitars now play it fully palm-muted, and the bass helps convey a sense of open space by continuing a sustaining/accenting pattern underneath. At measure 9, open the palm mute and let the music rage!

The chorus moves to B♭, the tritone of E. The high-pitched harmonic "noise" is produced by striking the middle strings at natural harmonic nodes on or around the third fret. Lay your third finger flat across strings 2–4, just lightly above the metal fret itself (or a little on the high side of it), and pick. The exact pitches aren't as important as the general quality created here. At the end of measure 14, we see a slide up from B♭5 to D♭5. Taken together, the root movement looks like E (the tonal center of the verse)–B♭–D♭, and suggests an overall E diminished seventh tonality (E–G–B♭–D♭).

33 Featured Guitars:
Gtr. 4   meas. 1-20

34 Slow Demos:
Gtr. 4   meas. 13-14

Fig. 15

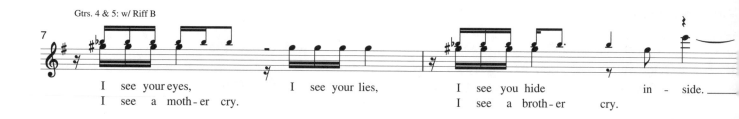

Gtrs. 4 & 5: w/ Riff B

I see your eyes,   I see your lies,   I see you hide   in-side.
I see a moth-er cry.   I see a broth-er cry.

Gtr. 1: w/ Riff A, 2 times

What goes a-round comes a-round. Now it's your time.   How long can you hide?   How long can you lie?

How long can you live with your soul-bleed?   How long can you life with your soul?

Chorus

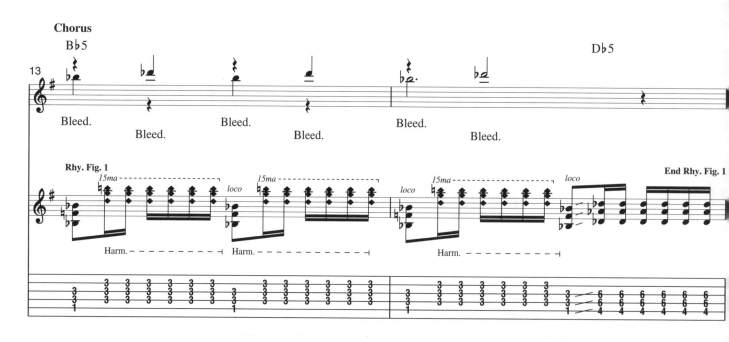

Bb5

Bleed.   Bleed.   Bleed.   Bleed.
Bleed.   Bleed.   Bleed.

Db5

Rhy. Fig. 1   15ma   loco   15ma   loco   15ma   loco   End Rhy. Fig. 1

Harm.   Harm.   Harm.

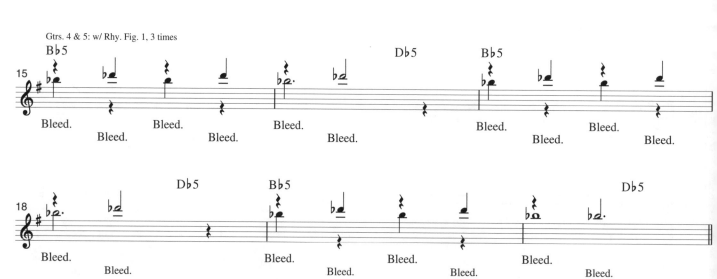

Gtrs. 4 & 5: w/ Rhy. Fig. 1, 3 times

Bb5   Db5   Bb5

Bleed.   Bleed.   Bleed.   Bleed.   Bleed.
Bleed.   Bleed.   Bleed.   Bleed.   Bleed.

Db5   Bb5   Db5

Bleed.   Bleed.   Bleed.   Bleed.
Bleed.   Bleed.   Bleed.   Bleed.

LOCO

Words by B. Dez Fafara
Music by Miguel Rascon, Rayna Foss, and Mike Cox

Figure 16–Intro

Coal Chamber formed in L.A. in the spring of 1994, which was about the same time that other bands like Korn and Deftones were honing their sound in similar rehearsal spots in Orange County and Sacramento, respectively. Mixing hardcore, goth, hip-hop, and punk influences with ultra-low tuning, Coal Chamber recorded a self-produced demo and set out on an aggressive street-level publicity campaign. Word of mouth spread, and soon they were packing shows at well-known Hollywood clubs such as the Whiskey A Go-Go and The Roxy. When Dino Cazares of Fear Factory and Ross Robinson simultaneously brought the band's demo to the attention of Roadrunner Records in the fall of 1995, a deal was offered. But just as things were on the rise, vocalist Dez Fafara quit the group unexpectedly. His less-than-understanding girlfriend demanded it, and Dez agreed—until one day when friend and guitarist "Meegs" Rascon knocked on his door again. None of the singers had worked out, and Meegs was asking Dez to rejoin the group. From that point, there was no looking back. Coal Chamber's self-titled debut album was released in 1997. "Loco" is the opening cut, as well as the standout track that graced the band's original demo.

The preferred tuning of Coal Chamber is that of a seven-string guitar (strings 2–7) on a six-string. This is similar to Soulfly's standard tuning down two and a half steps, except for the second string, which is a half step higher. Rather than view the strings as standard with this half-step exception, however, try looking at it like a seven-string for a moment. Strings 1–5 are as a standard-tuned guitar missing its high E string. Then simply add the ultra-low B string underneath. Since this tuning is viewed as an altered tuning and not any sort of slack tuning, we simply notate the pitches exactly as they sound.

 7-String Tuning on 6-String: B-E-A-D-G-B

This tune uses a semi-clean tone for the opening. I selected the POD clean, but cranked the drive (gain) up enough to get just the right amount of grit happening on strong pick attacks. Measures 1–2 bounce between unison Bs on the first and second strings. Measures 3–4 drop the fretted B one half step to A#, and the rhythmic quality of the note pattern emerges clearly. For the best tone, your picking should be determined by the physical locations of the strings, and *not* the rhythm. Pick all notes on the second string with downstrokes and all notes on the first string with upstrokes. In the distant background (mixed quietly with added delay), Gtr. 1 plays octaves that echo the dominant B to A# motion in Gtr. 2. The tonal center throughout is B.

At measure 17, the heaviness begins. Gtrs. 3 and 4 enter on a low, sustained B5 power chord to set the mood. After an extended pause, the vocal cue "pull" signals for the proverbial "all hell" to break loose. The following riff primarily utilizes the notes B–C#–D, then adds G–F# in measure 18; this riff first appears to shape up as B natural minor (B–C#–D–E–F#–G–A). However, closer inspection reveals the tonal center draws our ear up to C#, not the open B, thus creating the sound of C# Locrian (C#–D–E–F#–G–A–B). It's a matter of determining the correct root.

At its core, the riff is built upon a two-note B–C# motif that has been temporally displaced so as to fall against the underlying pulse differently with each repetition. In fact, it is quite similar to the rhythmic displacement seen earlier in this book. Rhythmically, the motif consists of a sixteenth and an eighth note, which, when added together, create a length total of *three* sixteenth-note subdivisions. Therefore, upon its repetition, we see the familiar "three-against-four" pattern emerge. (The three-against-four idea can incorporate any pattern that totals up to three sixteenth-note subdivisions—a similar rhythmic effect is conveyed whether the motif is made up of notes, rests, ties, or any combination of these.)

Featured Guitars:
Gtr. 2   meas. 1-16
Gtr. 4   meas. 17-25

Slow Demos:
Gtr. 2   meas. 1-4
Gtr. 4   meas. 20-23,
               24

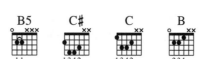

Fig. 16

Tune down as follows:
(low to high) B–E–A–D–G–B

Intro
Moderately ♩ = 118

w/ speaking

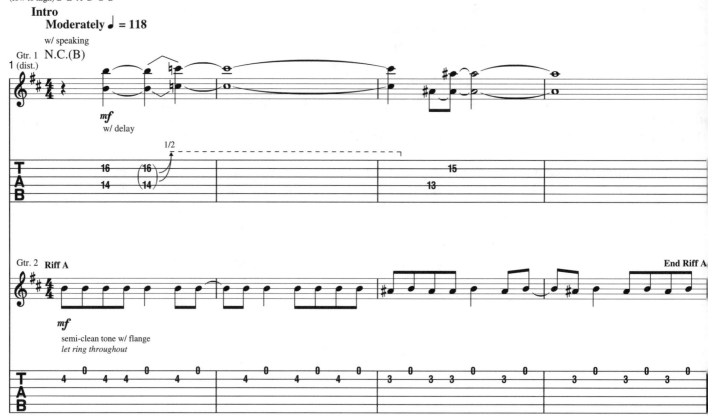

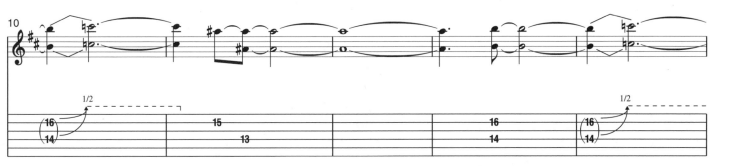

Gtr. 1 tacet

B5

Gtrs. 3 & 4
(dist.)

(cont. in notation)

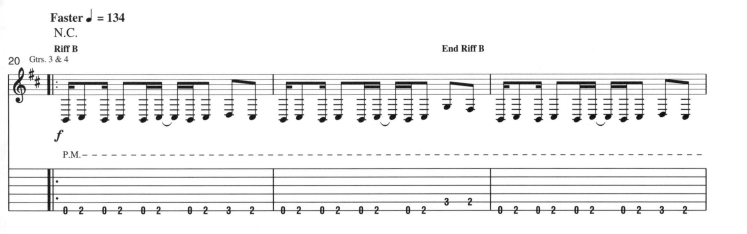

Pull!

rit.

Faster ♩ = 134
N.C.

Riff B

End Riff B

Gtrs. 3 & 4

f

P.M.

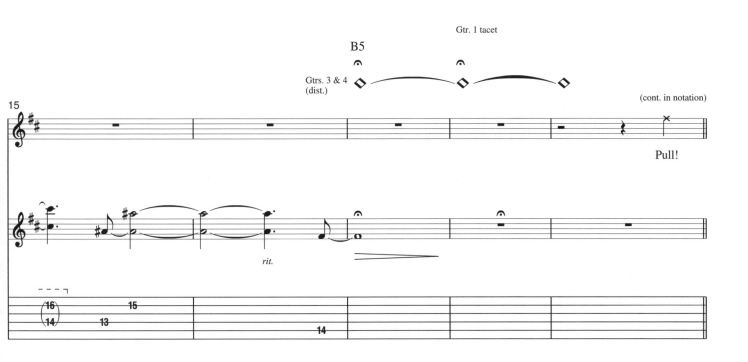

1., 3.
C#5 N.C.

2.
C#5 N.C. D5

4.

P.M.

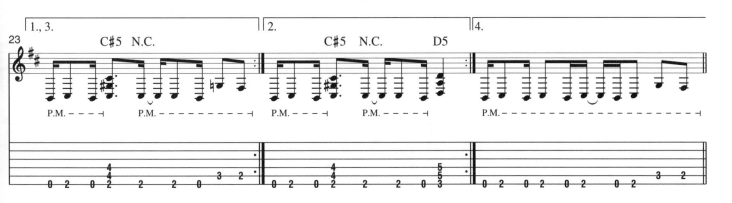

Figure 17–Verse, Chorus

Tension is apparent at the verse, as Gtr. 4 continues the main riff while Gtr. 3 opts for natural harmonic colorations before joining together at each fourth measure. The chorus breaks the verse's "steamroller" momentum with a series of chord accents and open space. Tonally, it borrows temporarily from the brighter, parallel major key (C♯ major) for its somewhat twisted quality. This is shifted chromatically down a half step to C major before falling to a sustained B5 and re-establishing the B tonal center.

38	**Featured Guitars:** Gtr. 4 meas. 1-17
39	**Slow Demos:** Gtr. 4 meas. 9-19

Fig. 17

*Lead vocal is doubled w/ slight variations ad lib (throughout).

56

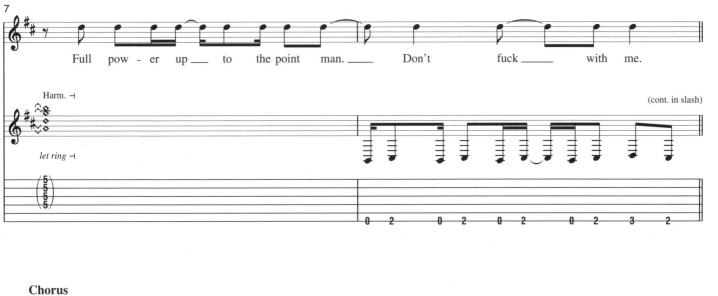

Full pow-er up___ to the point man.___ Don't fuck_____ with me.

Harm. ⊣

(cont. in slash)

let ring ⊣

Chorus

Gtrs.
3 & 4

C#

Lo - co, lo - co, lo - co,

C

lo - co. Mí lo - co, mí lo - co,

mí lo - co, mí lo - co._____ Pull!

Figure 18–Interlude, Bridge, Interlude

The interlude section is a chromatic passage centering on C#. Play with all down-strokes and fully palm muted. After four times, we head into the bridge—a gradually build-ing eight-measure structure. Over a B tonal center, Gtr. 4 plays octaves on strings 2 and 4. (Mute the third string with the side of your first finger.) The pitches B–C–B–C continue the chromatic motion (root–♭2nd–root–♭2nd) presented in the interlude, but on the longer time scale of one note per measure. The bridge ends with a rising diatonic sequence B–C–D–E, implying the B Phrygian mode.

The following interlude is a reprise of the intro figure, acting as a breakdown sec-tion. Here, the tempo abruptly shifts back to the opening, slower pace.

Fig. 18

Featured Guitars:
Gtr. 4   meas. 1-9
Gtr. 2   meas. 10-17
Gtr. 4   meas. 18

Slow Demos:
Gtr. 4   meas. 1, 2-9

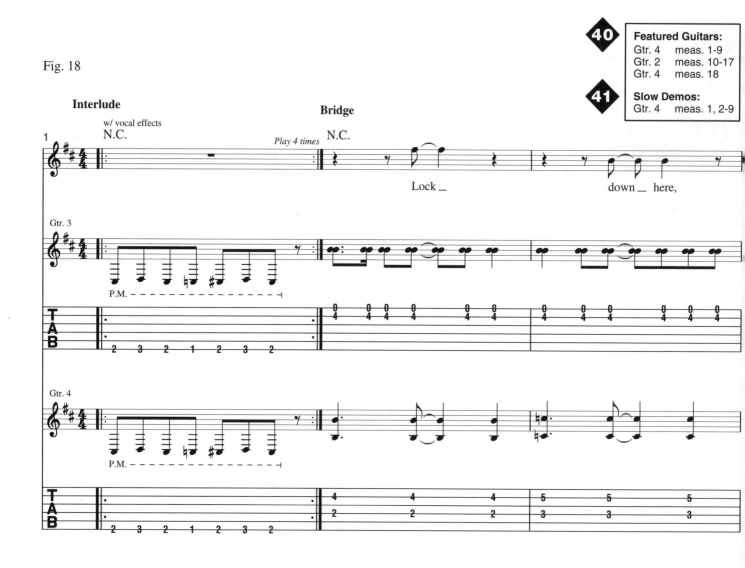

58

the sys - tem.   Full pow - er,   hit the main __ plan. __

Interlude

a Tempo
Gtr. 2: w/ Riff A, 2 times
Gtrs. 3 & 4 tacet

B5

Gtrs. 3 & 4 ◆

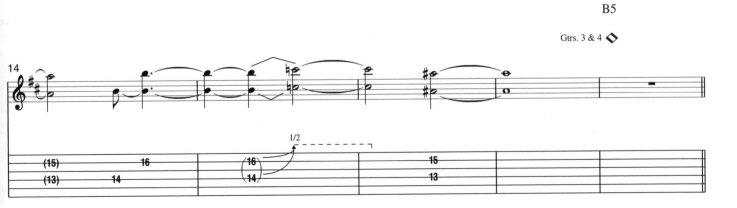

EDGECRUSHER

Music by Dino Cazeres, Raymond Herrera, and Christian Olde Wolbers
Lyrics by Burton C. Bell and Madchild

Figure 19–Intro, Verse, Pre-chorus, Chorus

Fear Factory was among the first to harness the crushing intensity of death metal and blend it with cold industrial electronic samples to express their bleak, futuristic vision of technology gone awry. Formed in Los Angeles in 1990 by Burton C. Bell (vocals), Raymond Herrera (percussion), and Dino Cazares (guitar), the band signed to Roadrunner Records and released their debut album in 1992. A second album, the six-track EP *Fear Is the Mind Killer,* added keyboards and further experimented with techno-metal fusion at the hands of remixers Rhys Fulber and Bill Leeb of Front Line Assembly. Then in 1994, bassist Andrew Shives was fired and replaced by Christian Olde Wolbers. *Demanufacture* in 1995 and non-stop tours with bands such as Korn and Biohazard would propel the group to greater and greater levels of success. The band continued their techno-industrial metal experiment with the 1997 remix EP *Remanufacture (Cloning Technology).* Their most recent sonic assault, *Obsolete,* was released in 1998. The disc chronicles the continuing saga of man vs. machine and takes things into previously uncharted territory.

Guitarist Dino Cazares explained, "I've always been a big fan of science fiction movies… Recording the new album was like asking ourselves, 'What would it sound like if we created the soundtrack to *The Terminator?'* We wanted to produce something very cinematic." The result is just that: their own complete musical sci-fi journey. Track 2, "Edgecrusher," is the part of the tale describing the faction of rebels fighting the current George Orwellian nightmare that society has become.

For full oppressive effect, the tuning is seven-string guitar down one whole step. So the lowest open string becomes the absolute pitch of A. Being a slacked variation of "standard" seven-string tuning, however, we still notate this at its unslacked pitch (low B) with the caveat that all notes will sound one step lower. To mimic seven-string tuning down a whole step on a six-string guitar, tune your strings 1–6 to the pitches of the seven-string's 2–7. (This is the same as Coal Chamber's tuning, except lowered one whole step across the board.) At first, it may seem a bit odd playing in this low a tuning. The notes are particularly difficult to hear accurate pitch, and low power chords sound downright dissonant. But don't worry. When it all comes together with the rest of the band, it works!

 7-String Down 1 Step: A–D–G–C–F–A–D
(6-string simulation: A–D–G–C–F–A)

Echoing the band's death metal influeces, the guitar tone here is scooped in the midrange. Additionally, loads of high, high-end are boosted. If you have a graphic EQ, boost everything between 8 kHz and 12 kHz, or even higher.

Based on a tonal center of B (absolute pitch A), C5 (♭II) leans on and falls to the tonic chord B5 (i), implying a B Phrygian tonality. The essential motif is C5–B5 followed by open B string palm mutes. Notice that this motif is played three times in measures 1–2, but on the second and third repetitions, we see that the C5 has been shifted earlier in time creating a syncopated-sixteenth feel. Pick down, down, down, down/up, down, etc. A chromatic passage at the end of measure 2 acts as a tag to finish up the phrase. Then measures 3–4 turn things around, replacing the C5–B5 move with its inversion: B5–C5. Try using your *second finger* to fret the B5 chords (not your first finger, as usual), then your first and third fingers will be available for C5. In this way, you can switch quickly between C5 and B5 without any position shifting. Guitars drop out suddenly at the verse, leaving bass and drums to form a foundation for the vocals.

The pre-chorus operates on a pair of tritone moves. The first lies between the open B (root of B5) and F at the sixth fret (root of F5) in measure 13. A second tritone interval then lies between D#5 and A5 in measure 14, followed by chromatic descending power chords which pull back down to B5. Standard alternate sixteenth picking would suggest a picking pattern here: *down, down/up, up/down, down*. However, I found the best replication of tone was enabled with a *down, down/up, down/up, down* pattern—overriding the standard picking format and opting instead for a pattern that reinforces the accented tritone power chords with consistent upstrokes.

The chorus barks over the riff delivered in the intro.

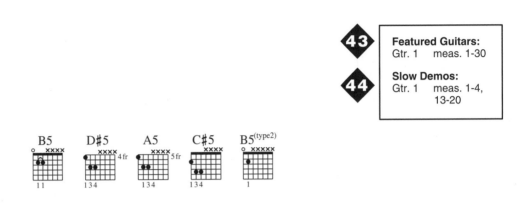

Featured Guitars:
Gtr. 1   meas. 1-30

Slow Demos:
Gtr. 1   meas. 1-4,
         13-20

Fig. 19

* 7 stg. gtr., tuned down one whole step:
  (low to high) A–D–G–C–F–A–D

* To simulate 6-stg. guitar, tune down to ADGCFA (low to high)
  and read the bottom six lines of tab staff.

Figure 20–Interlude

After a second verse and chorus, the interlude section pounds out a sequence of pure brutality. Fully unison rhythms accent beat 1, the "and" of beat 2 and its following sixteenth-note subdivision, and the "and" of 3. Slight deviations in measures 4, 6, and 8 are likewise played verbatim by drums and bass as well as guitar.

At measure 9, half-step moves back and forth between E (4th) and D♯ (major 3rd) dominate. Together with the B5–C5 chords in measure 12, this four-measure meltdown adds up to a B Phrygian-dominant scale (B–C–D♯–E–F♯–G–A). The rhythm consists of a three-note motif. The first note is three sixteenth-note subdivisions; the second note is three sixteenth-note subdivisions; the third note is two sixteenth-note subdivisions. The entire two-beat motif repeats with the pitches reversed in beats 3–4 of each measure.

Measures 13–16 spin out a new variation while still maintaining the same rhythmic premise. Here, each measure now ends with the same B5–C5–B5 sequence we had earlier at the end of measure 12. The front half of each measure is also bolstered up to power chords, rather than single notes, and the first note each time moves chromatically down from G5 to F♯5 to F5 to E5.

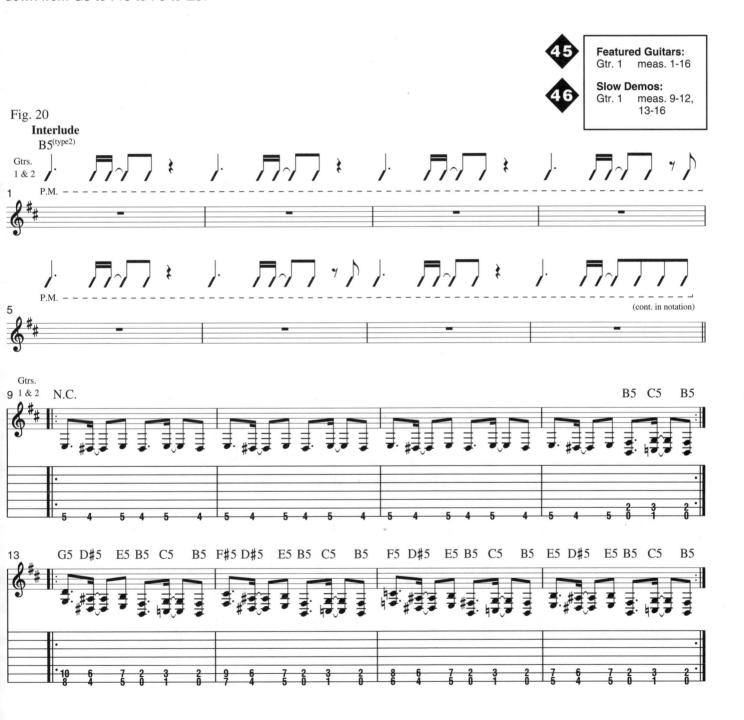

Fig. 20

45 Featured Guitars:
Gtr. 1   meas. 1-16

46 Slow Demos:
Gtr. 1   meas. 9-12, 13-16

COME ORIGINAL

Music by Nicholas Hexum and Aaron Wills
Words by Nicolas Hexum and Doug Martinez

Figure 21–Intro, Chorus, Verse, Chorus

The band 311 formed in 1990 in Omaha, Nebraska, blending a range of styles including rap, hard rock, funk, reggae, and hip-hop. The unusual name of the group reportedly arose, as the story goes, from the time their friend and former guitarist Jim Watson was caught skinnydipping—the police code for indecent exposure was "311." After doing three self-released recordings in Omaha (*Dammit!, Unity, Hydroponic*), the quintet moved to Van Nuys, California, and teamed up with producer Eddy Offord (Yes). Composed of Douglas Martinez ("Sa") on vocals and scratches, Aaron Wills ("P-Nut") on bass, Chad Sexton on drums, Tim Mahoney on guitar, and Nick Hexum on guitar and vocals, the group landed a deal with Capricorn Records (a Warner Bros. label) and released their debut, *Music*, in 1993. For their second release, *Soundsystem*, 311 took their time and were ultimately rewarded with a triple-platinum success. The first single from 1995's *Soundsystem*, was "Come Original."

This rap-rock style with urban rhythms, crunchy guitars, and tight punky melodies is admittedly a bit of a stretch for modern "metal," but it clearly holds down the hard rock side of modern guitar. The tuning is standard. You may need to re-string with a lighter gauge set for this tuning or take other setup precautions if you are using extra heavy strings.

 Standard Tuning: E–A–D–G–B–E

The tone is midrange crunch. I dialed up the POD to the rectified setting (MESA/Boogie simulation), cranked the midrange, pushed the treble up a bit, and backed off the low end. You'll want a thick, heavy distortion, but not over-saturated—you need to be able to stop the strings quickly and quietly for tight-sounding rests.

The tune opens with a Dsus2/A chord. This is a D chord in which the major 3rd tone has been supplanted by a 2nd, offering its characteristic suspended quality. The A note in the bass (the lowest note in the chord) helps to give the chord a thicker, fatter quality.

Now let's consider the rhythm. Notice that the chord strikes on the first and fourth sixteenth-note subdivisions of beat 1 and the upbeat of beat 2 are exactly the same faire as found in the interludes of "Edgecrusher" and "From This Day"—both heavier applications, but similar nonetheless in construction.

After Dsus2/A, a "super-syncopated" line skips down the D Lydian mode (D–E–F♯–G♯–A–B–C♯). To best maintain rhythmic momentum, pick down/up, up, up, up, up, up, up/down.

When the band kicks into full gear at measure 9, it's a chorus we hear first. The progression G5–B5–A5–A♭5, set against the established tonal center of D, gives us a IV–vi–V progression with the Ab5 acting as a chromatic passing chord. Notice the tension created as it temporarily argues with the surrounding chords.

Play with tight, fast picking motions on the chords, stopping the strings completely with both hands on each of the short, sixteenth rests. Alternate picking suggests a down/up, up, up, up, down/up, up, up, up pattern. After you get the hang of that, however, try it with all downstrokes. This is a bit tricky as the tempo is fairly quick for downstroked sixteenths.

An unusually short verse (four measures) maintains the exact same riff. Then it's back for another chorus. In a sense, though, you can regard this entire section as a single chorus with "subparts." This creative writing style—mixing up common song structures and making songs less predictable—is clearly a 311 strong point and signature element of the band's style.

Fig. 21

Chorus

come o - rig - i - nal, you got to come o - rig - i - nal. All en - ter - tain - ers, come o - rig - i - nal. You got to

come o - rig - i - nal, you got to come o - rig - i - nal. All en - ter - tain - ers, hear why. 1. To

Verse

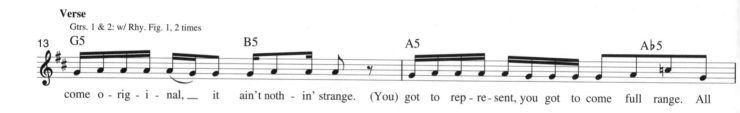

come o - rig - i - nal, __ it ain't noth - in' strange. (You) got to rep - re - sent, you got to come full range. All

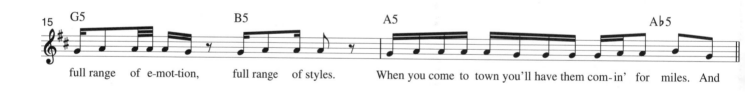

full range of e-mot-tion, full range of styles. When you come to town you'll have them com-in' for miles. And

Chorus

come o - rig - i - nal, you got to come o - rig - i - nal. All en - ter - tain - ers, come o - rig - i - nal. You got to

come o - rig - i - nal, you got to come o - rig - i - nal. All en - ter - tain - ers, hear why.

Figure 22–Verse, Rap Verse

Immediately on the heels of the last section, another four-measure verse breaks in. This time, however, the rhythm of the progression is altered as the song unfolds—another break with tradition. From B5 in the second phrase, we then walk down diatonically to E5 for a little breather as P-Nut takes over with some funky slap bass riffs.

As the vocal rapping begins, guitars initially offer sporadic offbeat accents, eventually building up to a full-scale rhythmic assault throughout measures 13–16. Tonal variance is denied. Stay right on E5 the entire time.

50

Featured Guitars:
Gtr. 1   meas. 1-16

51

Slow Demos:
Gtr. 1   meas. 1-6,
            13-16

Fig. 22

Figure 23–Interlude, Rap Verse, Interlude, Outro-Chorus

This melodic interlude section functions effectively like a solo, but involves the entire band in a new structural element. Gtrs. 1 and 2 enters on octaves, playing the note-pairs E/B, D/A, G/B, F#/A, and spelling out the implied progression E–D–G–F#m. (E/B is Em's root-5th, D/A is D's root-5th, G/B is G's root-3rd, and F#/A is F#m's root-♭3rd.)

After two times, Gtrs. 3 and 4 are added on a harmony line, also in octaves. Now we can see that the progression begins not with E, but Em, as Gtrs. 3 and 4 add the crucial third tone—in this case G. The next chord, D, now becomes a Dmaj7 due to the inclusion of C#. But G and F#m remain harmonically unaffected as the new parts simply add 5ths to the chords.

Next in line is another rapped verse on E5 for eight measures, followed by a breakdown interlude with pristine, reverb-drenched clean guitar strums. A slight chorus also enhances the tone. Here the chords are simply the top three strings of the same progression seen earlier in the chorus. Now with the inclusion of 3rds, we have full triads instead of power chords, and the progression becomes G–Bm–Am–A♭. For the outro-chorus, heavy guitars enter in tandem with the clean-verb guitar.

52 **Featured Guitars:**
Gtr. 1   meas. 1-2
Gtr. 3   meas. 3-6
Gtr. 1   meas. 7-14
Gtr. 5   meas. 15-18
Gtr. 1   meas. 19-20

53 **Slow Demos:**
Gtr. 1   meas. 1-2
Gtr. 3   meas. 3-4
Gtr. 5   meas. 15-17

Fig. 23

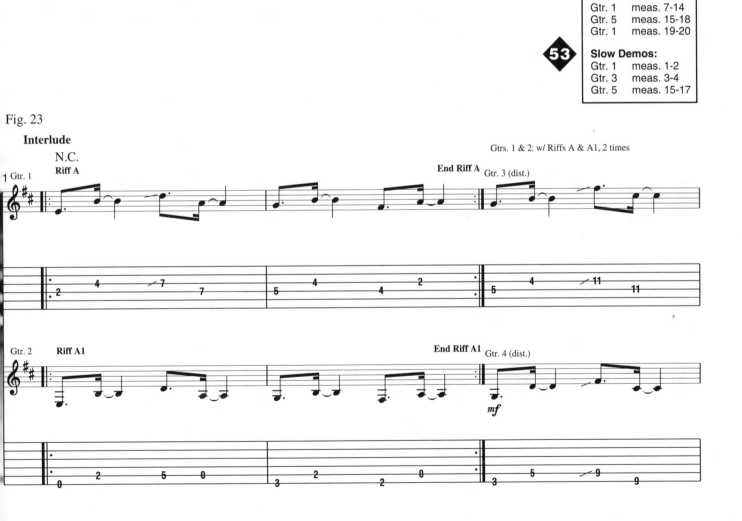

Interlude

Gtrs. 1 & 2: w/ Riffs A & A1, 2 times

Rap Verse

One, two, three, four.

4. Ev-'ry-thing we do, we got-ta come o-rig-i-nal. Put your hand up in the air and pre-pare for bat-tle.

Sit u-pon the rhy-thm like a tire u-pon a rim. We do it non-stop and then we do it a-gain.

Some of them whine and some them bitch. They can-not do it, nev-er switch. Com-in' up from the heart and de-liv-ered with a wild pitch.

Sit up on top of the rhy-thm like a wild stal-li-on. This is the ru-ling sys-tem.

Interlude

Outro-Chorus

Come o-rig-i-nal, you got to come o-rig-i-nal. All en-ter-tain-ers, come o-rig-i-nal. You got to

PARDON ME

Words and Music by Brandon Boyd, Michael Einziger, Alex Katunich, Jose Pasillas II and Chris Kilmore

Figure 24–Intro, Pre-Verse, Verse, Chorus

Incubus was formed in 1991 inside a garage in Calabasas, California. Brandon Boyd (vocals), Mike Einziger (guitars), Dirk Lance (bass), Jose Pasillas (drums), and DJ Chris Kilmore (turntables) developed their following at Hollywood area gigs and released their own independent recording, *Fungus-Amongus*. Soon the group got signed to Immortal/Epic and put out a six-song EP of demos entitled *Enjoy Incubus*. A European tour with Korn came next. In 1997, their first full-length album *S.C.I.E.N.C.E.* was released and more touring followed with Korn, Black Sabbath, Limp Bizkit, Ozzy Osbourne, 311, and others. The band joined forces with co-producer Scott Litt (R.E.M., Nirvana) for their next effort, *Make Yourself*, released in 1999. According to band front man Brandon Boyd, they have found "happiness and contentment in being a hard rock band that didn't feel the need to be the hardest, with the most strings tuned down." In fact, "Pardon Me" is played in standard tuning—unusual for a band surrounded by this much heaviness. But that is at least one element that helps to set this group apart. Brandon describes their style as embodied in *Make Yourself* as "Heavy, melodic, diverse, plugged-in yet detached, thought-provoking, thought-out spontaneous, observational, silly, and slightly intelligent."

The inspiration for "Pardon Me" came to Brandon while browsing through a bookstore and finding an article on spontaneous human combustion: "an old guy's legs and shoes, perfectly intact... then, right around his knee area was just a pile of charred ashes... The image struck a chord, so I wrote a song about it."

The opening portion of the tune is dominated by a clean guitar tone with smooth volume swells and thick delay. You'll need a volume pedal to achieve this effect. Also, set a delay to produce an echo in the neighborhood of 400 milliseconds and with a regeneration set to allow roughly four or five echos before fading off entirely. Strike the first chord with the volume pedal fully backed off, and then rock forward. This completely eliminates the initial attack of the pick for a smooth swell. Then back off fully and strum the second chord at approximately the "and" of beat 4—a half beat sooner than you want the chord swell to start. The delay will cover up the momentary period of silence that is created there, and allow each chord swell to connect with the next fluently.

Finger the C♯m7 chord using your third finger on the lowest note, C♯ (string 5), your first finger on E (string 4), and your fourth finger on B (string 3). An open B string rings in unison to help create a more continuous, smooth quality. Then, without moving any other fingers, simply lift your third finger to change the bass note to an open A. Over a C♯ root, the chord tones are: root, minor 3rd, and minor 7th. Over the A root, they become: root, 5th, suspended 2nd. In the last two beats of measure 4, strike just the higher portion of Asus2 without changing any fingerings. The key is C♯m, which places the C♯m7 as a tonic chord and Asus2 as a type of ♭VI chord.

Kick on full distortion at measure 9 for the heavier interpretation of the same progression. Here we have second inversion-slash chords which, due to the 5th in the bass, offer an extra thick quality—at least partially making up for the fact that standard tuning is relatively "thin" by modern heavy rock standards. C♯m7 is replaced with C♯5/G♯; Asus2 becomes Asus2/E, and the final "top portion" of Asus2 is transformed to E5, anchoring it exclusively to the E note of the chord and forgoing any attachment to A. Pick each quarter note with a downstroke and each pair of eighth notes with down/up strums.

The verse is way out there. Change back to the clean tone with volume pedal and delay. A series of swelled jazz chords give an air of disconnectedness from the tight bass/drum accompaniment with its interspersed accent points. Use the pick held between your thumb and index finger to strike the lowest string of each chord, and the remaining fingers 2, 3, and 4 can pluck each of the higher strings. This is called "hybrid picking." The first chord, G#m7(no3rd), is a G#m9 shape with the second string omitted. Fret it with your second finger on string 5, first finger on string 4, then barre across strings 1–3 with your third finger laying flat. You simply avoid plucking the second string to keep it from sounding. The second chord, B/E, is formed with your first finger on string 5, second finger on string 4, then barre across strings 1–3 with your fourth finger, again avoiding the sounding of string 2 due to your right hand plucking technique. Notice that these chords are essentially a mirror image of the original C#m7–Asus2, except shifted up an interval of a 5th. As with the original progression, here too, only the bass note changes and all other pitches are common tones.

The third chord is D#7(#5). This is a D#7 shape (no 5th) with an added open B string acting as a #5th. Another name for this chord is D#aug7—that is, a D# augmented chord with a dominant 7th. This hangs for two measures to complete and close a full, four-measure phrase.

We see the next natural four-measure phrase depart from the norm—a simple repetition. Here, a rest/accent figure enters, followed by the repeating delay effect. This wholly unexpected break sets everything into limbo. Yet, the natural four-measure phrase again closes with another long, swelled chord pause. This time it's a D6/9 chord formed by playing a D5 power chord shape along with open strings high E (9th) and B (6th).

A third four-measure phrase mirrors the previous one, starting once again with the rest/accent and delay repeats. The closing chord is another form of B/E. Use your second finger on string 1, first finger on string 3, and fourth finger on string 4, also touching and lightly muting string 5. Strum across all six strings to sound the chord.

A fourth four-measure phrase ends the bizarre journey that is the verse. This time we forgo any accent (and its attendant echoes) and simply rest for the first two measures. Kick back on the distortion for the last two measures and buildup into the chorus on an A5 power chord. Relative to the tonal center of C#, A5 is the bVI chord.

At first, it seems the chorus is similar to the earlier heavy guitar section with the same opening chords C#5/G#–A5/E progression. But it departs significantly. In measure 34, A5/E rises immediately to B5/F# (bVII chord), then back down to Asus2. Then the rifflike E5–F#5 powers through the end of measure 35 and into measure 36. This also gives us a four-measure phrase element, which is repeated for the chorus' second line.

The third phrase element (measures 41–44) alters the progression again, staying longer on A5/E and delaying the entrance of B5/F#. A string of unison Bs dominates the final measure of this phrase. Stop the lower strings here by lifting your fingering and fretting only B on string 3.

The fourth and final phrase is a repetition of the third, except that it pulls the ending E5–F#5 riff portion from the beginning phrases of the chorus—so it is in fact a hybrid of the two preceding ideas.

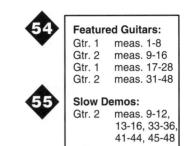

Featured Guitars:
Gtr. 1   meas. 1-8
Gtr. 2   meas. 9-16
Gtr. 1   meas. 17-28
Gtr. 2   meas. 31-48

Slow Demos:
Gtr. 2   meas. 9-12,
          13-16, 33-36,
          41-44, 45-48

Fig. 24

Intro

Moderately ♩ = 152

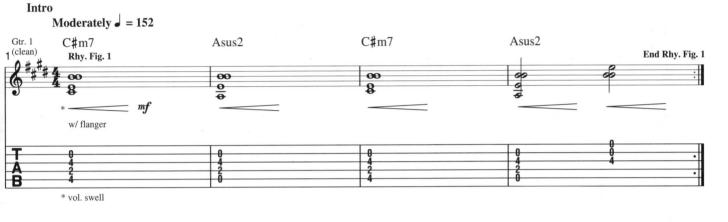

* vol. swell

Pre-Verse

Half-time feel

Gtr. 1: w/ Rhy. Fig. 1, 2 times

Par - don me, ____ while __ I burst. _____

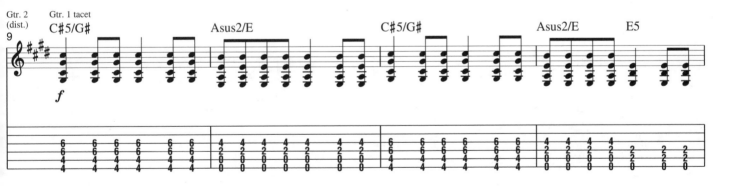

End Half-time feel

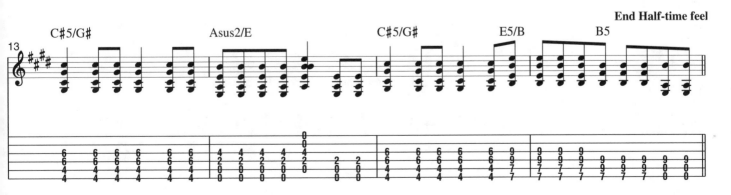

TESTIFY

Written and Arranged by Rage Against the Machine

Figure 25–Intro, Verse, Chorus

Rage Against the Machine came together in 1991, playing their first "gig" at a friend's living room in Orange County, California. Vocalist Zack de la Rocha and guitarist Tom Morello joined with Tom's childhood friend and bassist Tim Commerford, then added drummer Brad Wilk to complete the quartet. The new group's own brand of heavy, funk-rap rebellion rock first hit tape in 1992 with their self-produced, twelve-song demo cassette. After selling over 5,000 copies and attracting a large L.A. area following, RATM caught the interest of Epic Records and released their self-titled debut album in 1992. It was certified platinum less than two years later. The follow up release, *Evil Empire*, in 1994, would climb the charts even faster, entering the Billboard Top 200 Albums chart at #1 and scoring a hit single with "Bulls on Parade." Their third effort is *The Battle of Los Angeles*. Now with all three albums certified double-platinum, RATM is a significant modern rock movement in itself.

"Testify" is the lead cut from *The Battle of Los Angeles* and presents the band doing their own hard, funk-rap metal rendition of a walking, Texas blues-style riffing approach. For tone, I selected the POD's "Brit Hi Gain" setting (Marshall emulation). The tuning is Drop D.

 Drop D Tuning: D–A–D–G–B–E

According to Tom, the intro is actually performed by pulling off to the low open D string once every two measures and using his signature toggle-switching technique to create the rhythmic aspect while rocking back and forth with his wah pedal. A strong flange effect was then added on mixdown. The sounding harmonics, then, are actually a byproduct of the wah pedal accentuating certain harmonic frequencies—they are not played as notes per se.

Nevertheless, in order to achieve the best replication of this section, I chose a different tact, playing the actual sounding natural harmonics rather than emulating Tom's trademark toggle-switching technique. In any case, the overall super-heavy flange is clearly the dominant aspect here, regardless of how you choose to create the notes themselves. First, I ran in a flanger effect pedal set for a high regeneration and high delay amount. The output of the flanger then went into a Digitech XP100 "whammy pedal" set to wah patch 06. I picked the natural harmonics on the low D string in a sextuplet rhythm (six notes per beat).

The lowest harmonic is found at the fourth fret—directly above the metal fret itself, not the fret space. Lightly touch the string at that point with your middle finger and pick to produce the pitch F♯, two octaves plus a major 3rd above the open D string. The mid harmonic is found just slightly higher that the point above the third metal fret and produces the pitch A, two octaves plus a 5th above the open D string. The highest harmonic is found roughly another half inch down the string at fret 2.6. This produces the pitch C, two octaves plus a ♭7th above the open D string.

Over the tonal center of D, these three notes add up to a D7 chord. To play the intro using this harmonic method, slide your middle finger between these harmonics as indicated while picking a fast sextuplet pattern.

The main riff first appears in measures 9–12, lead by a Texas-blues inspired Dm7 chord on beat 1. This is followed by single-note riffing drawn from the D minor pentatonic scale (D–F–G–A–C). In measures 10–12, some of the single notes have added 5ths, transforming them into power chords. Simply lay your finger flat across two strings to accomplish this. The main riff also functions later as the bedrock of the chorus.

The verse harkens back to the intro technique—whichever method you choose to accomplish it by. In any case, the pattern is simplified into a repeating two-measure pattern.

Fig. 25

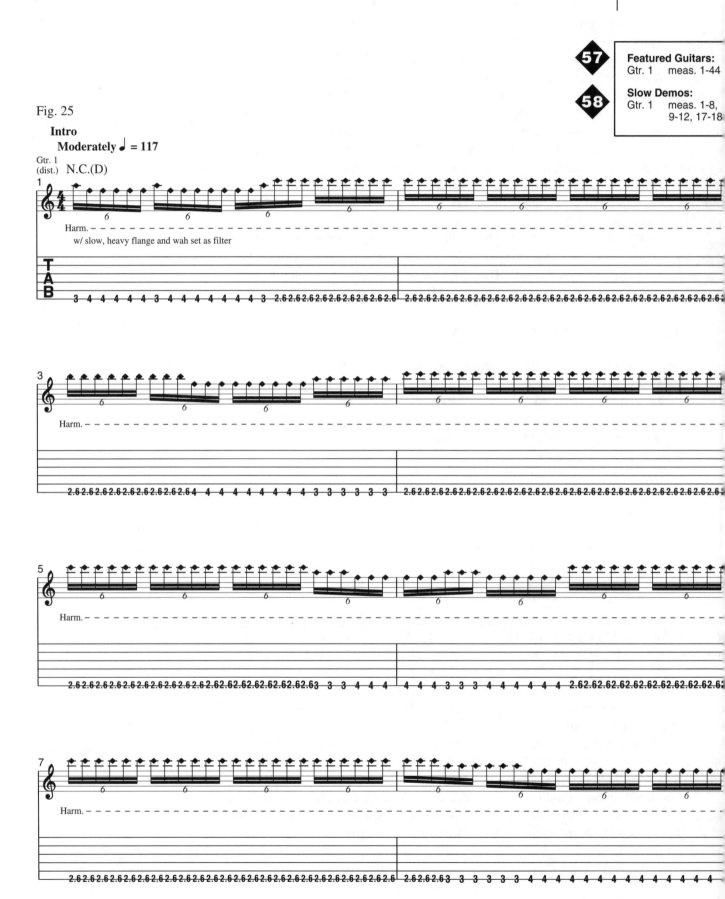

Figure 26–Bridge, Guitar Solo, Interlude

The bridge section draws strongly from a '70s funk influence, using a clean guitar playing sixteenth-note rhythms. The notes here are simply octave Ds. For a true funk approach, make sure your fretting hand fingers touch and hold mute strings 2 and 4 so you can whack at the strings freely without creating any unwanted open string noise. Your picking hand should attack the strings quickly on both the down and upstrokes, so it sounds more like single, solid attacks and not like strumming. Try to sound all the strings nearly simultaneously with each pick.

The solo is another highly rhythmic endeavor. Effect-wise, this employs an envelope filter, which I achieved by setting the XP100 whammy pedal to patch 11. Measures 9, 11, 13, and 15 are played with the pedal fully forward (which delays the "swell" longer), while measures 10, 12, 14, and 16 are played with the pedal fully backed off (which allows the "swell" to happen almost instantly). Maintain a standard sixteenth-note alternate picking format here to best execute the rhythm. All notes falling on downbeats or upbeats should be played with downstrokes. All notes falling on second or fourth sixteenth-note subdivisions should be played with upstrokes.

The interlude in measures 17–24 is straightahead, classic heavy metal—an interesting choice considering the clean funk that came just before. The progression here implies a D natural minor tonality with F5–C5–D5 (♭III–♭VII–i), played in big, long power chords. Rock out!

Guitar Solo

*Digitech XP100, patch 11, + = fully forward, o = fully backed off.

Interlude

WELCOME TO THE FOLD

Words and Music by Richard Patrick

Figure 27–Intro, Verse, Chorus

Richard Patrick was the lead guitarist of the electronic-industrial band Nine Inch Nails for their original touring lineup. Shortly after NIN finished its first tour in the early 90s, he met Brian Liesegang through a mutual friend, and the two began to record heavy, electro-industrial rock together. With Richard on vocals, guitars, bass, and drums, and Brian on programming, guitars, keyboards, and drums, their debut album, *Short Bus*, was released on Reprise in 1995 and quickly went gold, driven by the successful single, "Hey Man, Nice Shot." Brian departed in 1997, but Patrick continued on, and his next album, *Title of Record*, was released in 1999. The current touring lineup consists of Richard plus Gene Lenardo, Steve Gillis, and Frank Cavanaugh.

The tuning for "Welcome to the Fold" is drop A. Keep strings 1–5 in standard tuning, then simply lower the sixth string all the way down to a phat, flappy A. This results in octave intervals between strings 5 and 6.

 Drop A Tuning: A–A–D–G–B–E

The tone is fairly dark and thick. Largely, this is due to the tuning itself; I simply ran through the POD through its rectified preset (MESA/Boogie) with the bass up a bit, and the mid and treble flat (12 o'clock). Back your presence control off as well.

The hypnotic opening riff growls in octaves. Lay your index finger flat across strings 5-6 at the third fret (Cs), then hammer your third finger down at the fifth fret to sound octave Ds. Taken together, the pitches in this case, A–C–D, add up to a D minor pentatonic (D–F–G–A–C) tonality. Standard sixteenth-note alternate picking suggests a pattern of: *down, down/up, up, up* for each two beat motif.

After three times through the motif, a final slide up to octave Fs (♭3rds) in measure 2 breaks the pattern. Then this entire figure is repeated in measures 3–4 with a different ending tag, consisting of C (♭7th) accents set against low A (5th) palm mutes. These four measures make up Riff A—the main riff of the tune, functioning both as an intro and verse. Keep counting as you play along, or you may well get lost without vocal cues! Two repetitions act as the intro, then four full repetitions make up the verse.

The chorus opens up into a huge, cavernous space of sustaining low chord tones. The progression here is D–C–F–G, with one measure per chord. Of course, the low octaves only spell out the single notes rather than full chords (heck, not even power chords). But we can infer the chord tones from the vocal melody and the general tonal context. At measure 29, Gtrs. 2 and 3 enter, verifying our suspicions and filling out the chords with at least most of their missing tones. The progression is drawn from D minor. A brighter harmonic twist occurs upon each D chord, however. Whereas the tonic chord's natural diatonic state should be Dm, here we borrow momentarily from the parallel major key to give us a D major chord and brighten things up considerably.

Drop A tuning:
(low to high) A♭–A–D–G–B–E

Intro
Moderate Rock ♩ = 92

Gtrs. 1 & 2 (dist.)   N.C.(Dm)
(drums)   Riff A

Verse

Gtr. 1: w/ Riff A, 4 times
N.C.(Dm)

1. You take my mon-ey;   you think you're great. __

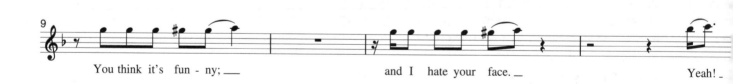

You think it's fun-ny; __   and I hate your face. __   Yeah! __

You got your Je-sus   and I got my space. __

You got your rea-sons,   and I got my case. __

84

Figure 28–Interlude, Bridge, Guitar Solo, Interlude

The interlude in measures 1–8 consists of a slide guitar melody played with a wah pedal over the main riff. This melody is made up of three notes, C–D–F# (♭7th–root–3rd), used in a rhythmically displaced fashion. To play slide guitar, place your slide over your third finger and lay it across the strings to touch them lightly at the fifth fret. Do not press down to the fretboard. Also, be careful to touch directly over the area of the metal fret itself and not the corresponding fret space. Pick the third string (C) and slide your entire hand up two frets to sound the next note, D. Then pick the second string (F#), followed by another D on string 3. You may rotate the slide slightly off the second string if necessary, to keep it from sustaining longer than needed.

The bridge is similar in feel to the chorus, but the chords are different. Here we see an A–D (V–I) chord motion applied four times.

A real guitar solo (gasp!) blasts in at measure 25. At first glance, this may appear to use the familiar box 1 A minor pentatonic shape. But in fact, the tonal center here is D, so we need to view it relative to underlying D shapes and scales. The solo opens with a three-against-four pattern at seventeenth position, as the notes F#–E–C# (3rd–2nd–♭7th) cascade against the pulse. Measure 26 then shifts down to the lower octave position for a quick sequence-based diatonic run. Superimpose the run over the D major chord shape at the fifth fret and you may immediately see how it relates to the underlying chord. The notes G–F#–E–D in beat 1 form tones 4–3–2–1 and seem to be drawn from D major. The next beat includes E–D–C–B, which form 2–1–♭7–6 relative to the D tonal center. Taken together, all the notes fit nicely into D Mixolydian. Beat 3 contrasts this with a bend up to F natural (minor 3rd) and then ends on D–A (root–5th).

Measures 27–28 dwell around C (♭7th) and continue with the established diatonic, scalar approach, ultimately ending on a low F# (major 3rd). Measure 29 rises up the scale, still D Mixolydian, throwing in a hint of three-against-four phrasing once again. Tremolo picking starts measure 30. Pick fast down/up/down/up throughout the length of the first note. This position seems to suggest the handy work of A minor pentatonic, but again, we are in D here. So, C is actually a minor 7th, D (root) bends up to the non-chord tone E (2nd), and back to land on an unresolved C (♭7th). Measures 31–32 harken back to the interlude melody to wind things down to a close.

At this point, the band cuts out and everything fades down to a whisper at the interlude (measure 33). Gtr. 3 enters with a clean tone playing tap harmonics. For the first note, hold E at the ninth fret, string 3, with your left hand and tap sharply with your right hand index finger exactly twelve frets higher (at the twenty-first fret), right on the metal fret itself. The sounding note will be a harmonic at the pitch that you tapped. For the next group of tap harmonics (measure 35), hold E with your left hand first finger and a high D with your second finger. Tap each exactly twelve frets higher and allow them to ring together.

Notice how the rhythm and note pattern changes in measure 39. This time, fret E with your first finger (string 3), high D with your second (string 1), and B with your fourth finger (string 2). Harmonically, this may look like an E7 chord, but keep in mind that this whole section is over a low A tonal center. That makes E a 5th, D a 4th, and B a 2nd. The overall harmonic implication is a set of sustaining 2nd and 4th suspensions. Gradually, amid tap harmonic variations, the interlude builds back to a raging fit of insanity.

64 Featured Guitars:
Gtr. 2 meas. 1-8
Gtr. 3 meas. 9-24
Gtr. 2 meas. 25-33
Gtr. 4 meas. 34-64

65 Slow Demos:
Gtr. 2 meas. 1-2,
25-32

Fig. 28

Interlude

Interlude

WHEN WORLDS COLLIDE

Lyrics by Spider
Music by Powerman 5000

Figure 29–Intro, Verse, Chorus, Verse, Chorus

Beginning in 1991, the Boston-based "action-rock" band Powerman 5000 started as a collaboration between vocalist Mike Cummings (aka "Spider")—younger brother of Rob Zombie (White Zombie, Rob Zombie)—and the rhythm section of Dorian Heartsong ("Dorian22") on bass and Al Pahanish ("Al3") on drums. By 1993, the full lineup also included Adam "12" Williams guitar and Jordan Cohen as percussionist. Later, a second guitarist, "M33," was added. Powerman's first commercial release was a self-produced, five-song cassette titled *A Private Little War*, which sold out its limited run of 500 copies within three weeks. They were then picked up by upstart indie label Curve of the Earth and recorded *True Force* in 1994, an EP done for a reported $600 and tracked in two days. Their first full-length release, *The Blood Splat Rating System*, followed, earning the band Best Metal, Best Rap Album, and Album of the Year in the local Boston Phoenix/WFNX Readers/Listeners Poll, and attracting the attention of the California-based, major label Dreamworks.

PM5K signed and moved west, releasing *Mega!! Kung Fu Radio* in 1997, with remixed versions of the *Blood Splat* material plus a few new tunes. After a year of cross-country touring with Korn, Limp Bizkit, Primus, Marilyn Manson, and Coal Chamber, the group returned to the studio in 1998 to begin recording *Tonight The Stars Revolt!*, with co-producers Sylvia Massey (Tool) and Ulrich Wild (White Zombie, Soundgarden). Released 1999, this can best be described as a "nostalgic look at the future," from a time long since passed (i.e., the early 1960s).

"When Worlds Collide" utilizes a slack tuning, down one half step. This is like standard tuning except all strings are lowered a half step across the board—also sometimes called "Eb tuning" since the low E string sounds the absolute pitch of Eb. Still, we regard and notate all pitches in the standard, unslacked pitches, so we can avoid renaming all the notes on the neck.

Down 1/2 Step: Eb–Ab–Db–Gb–Bb–Eb

For tone, I dialed the POD up to the "Brit Hi Gain" setting (Marshall), backed off the bass a little, and pushed up the mids and highs.

The song opens with a synth bass/vocal intro. Two pick scrapes signal the entering verse, where the synth bass begins with the song's central motif of a Db to G tritone move in the context of a syncopated eighth-note rhythm. Gtr. 1 enters in measure 10, essentially augmenting the bass line and filling it out with added Db octaves and b5th ones. Use your second, third, and fourth fingers to play the Db(b5), then your first finger available for the single-note G. Use all downstrokes in your picking. In each space left by Gtr. 1, a second guitar answers back quietly with a thin, brittle, and massively distort-ed tone.

Gtrs. 1 and 2 join together at measure 17, leading into the chorus. Here the chords G5–F5 (i–bVII) dominate the riff and cement the tonal center upon G. After three repetitions of the tight, one-measure motif, a chord move up to Bb5 signals the end of the four-measure phrase. Gtr. 1 opts for single notes, up an octave. Taken together, the chords G5, F5, and Bb5 add up to a G minor pentatonic tonality (G–Bb–C–D–F). Make sure you stop all the strings cleanly, using both hands, for each eighth rest. All chords are downstroked. The difficulty here lies in making accurate, smooth position shifts to effect the G5–F5 chord slides.

Verse 2 opens at a higher dynamic level than the first verse, with the guitar present right off the bat. At its mid point (measure 30), Gtr. 1 holds the tonic note G, adding a series of quick half-step bends. Pick only the first G here, then bend and release repeatedly to create the rhythmic quality.

At measure 41, the written repeat "D.S. al Fine" means to go back to the sign (%) and play until the "fine" (end). In other words, you go back and play the chorus.

Fig. 29

94

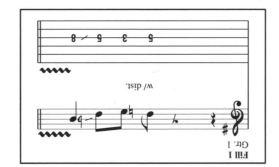

Verse
Gtrs. 1 & 2: w/ Riff A & A1, 2 times
27
Db(b5) N.C. Db(b5) N.C.
What is it real-ly that mo-ti-vates you? The need to fly or this fear to stop?
Gtr. 2: w/ Riff A1 (5 times)
31
Db(b5) N.C. Db(b5) N.C.
I'll go a-long, then you real-ize. When we get there I say nine of ten drop.
End Rhy. Fig. 2
1/2
Gtr. 1: w/ Riff A, 2 times
35
Db(b5) N.C. Db(b5) N.C.
Now who's the light and who is the dev-il? You can't de-cide so I'll be your guide.
39
Db(b5) N.C. Db(b5) N.C. G5 F5 G5 F5 G5
And one by one they will be hand cho-sen. Now this is what it's like when worlds col-lide!
1/2

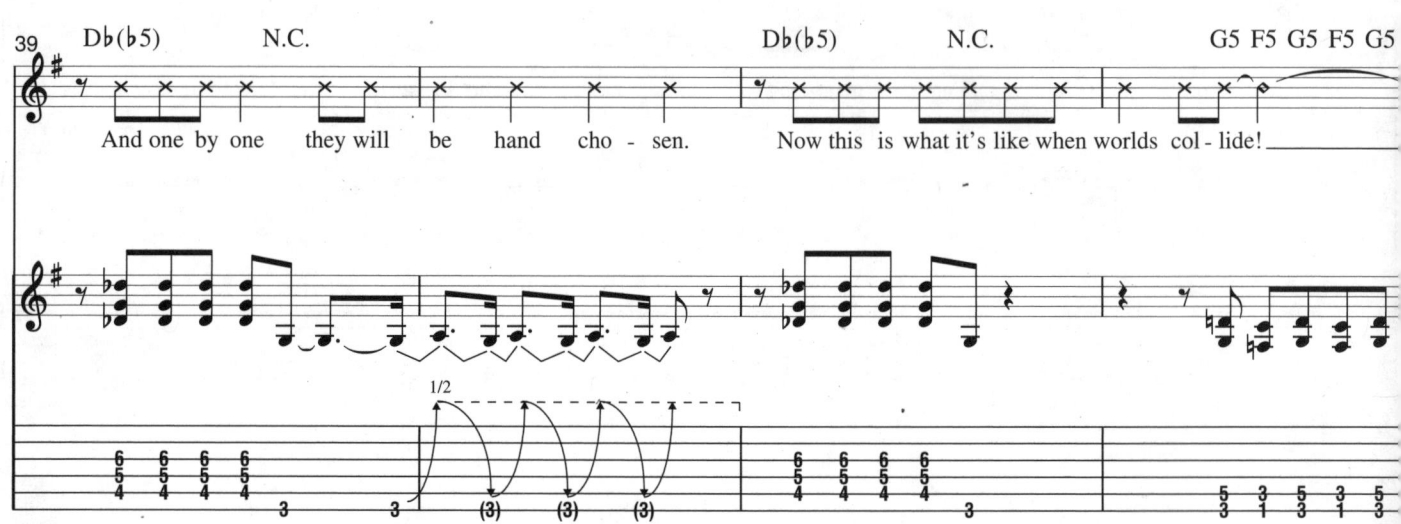

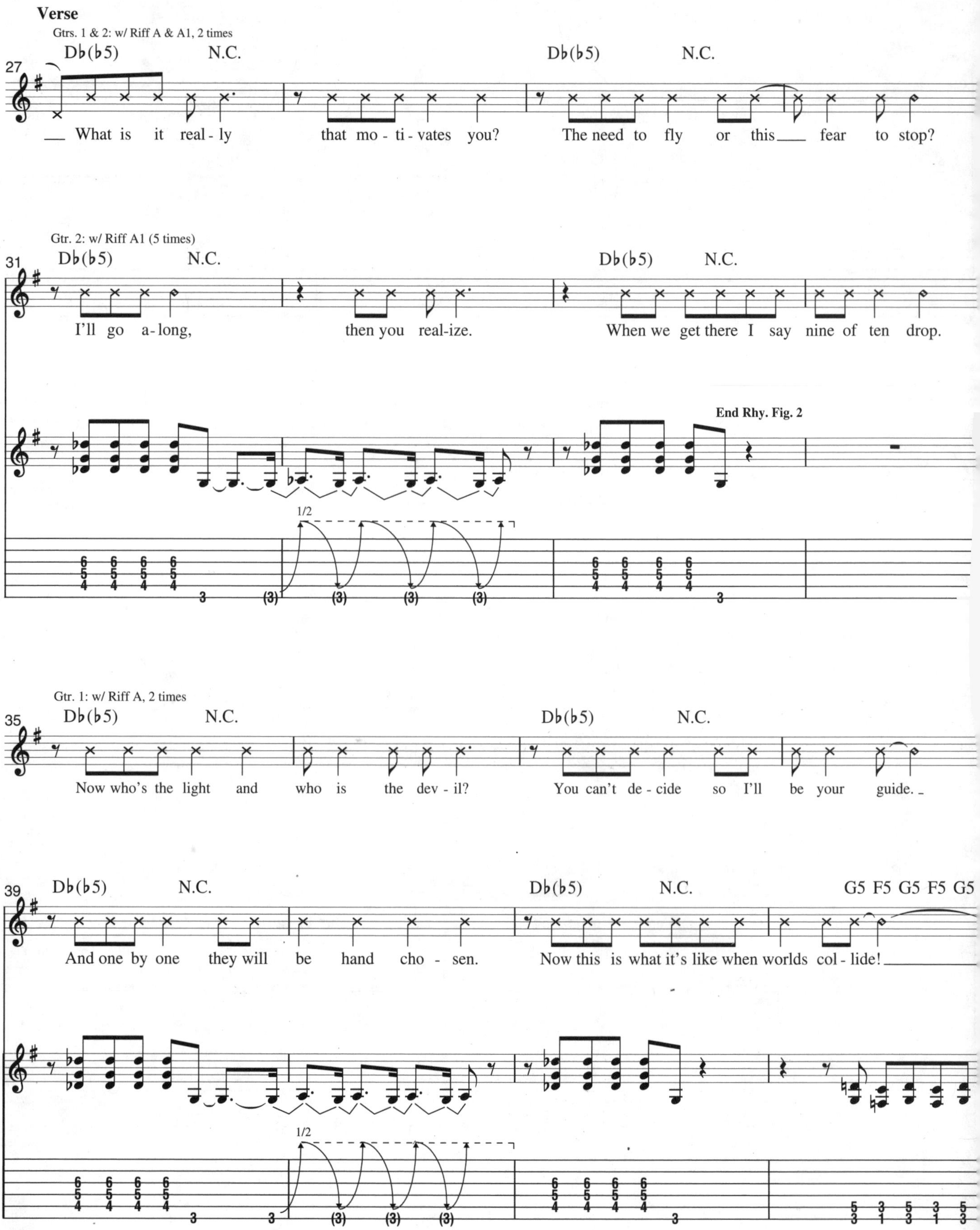